CONTENTS

POEMS 1974-1996

First published in 1997 by **Salzburg University** in its series:

SALZBURG STUDIES IN ENGLISH LITERATURE
POETIC DRAMA & POETIC THEORY
191

EDITORS: WOLFGANG GÖRTSCHACHER & JAMES HOGG

ISBN 3-7052-0085-2

INSTITUT FÜR ANGLISTIK UND AMERIKANISTIK
UNIVERSITÄT SALZBURG
A-5020 SALZBURG
AUSTRIA

Photographs by Elizabeth Carson. Sumi-ink paintings by Richard Lethen. Cover design by Stelios Ghikas.

Distributed by
Drake International Services
Market House, Market Place,
Deddington OXFORD OX15 0SF
England
Phone 01869 338240
Fax N°: 01869 338310

Distributed in the U.S.A. by
International Specialised Book Services Inc.
5804 NE Hassalo Street
Portland
Oregon 97213-3644
Phone 503.287.3093
Fax: 503.280.8832

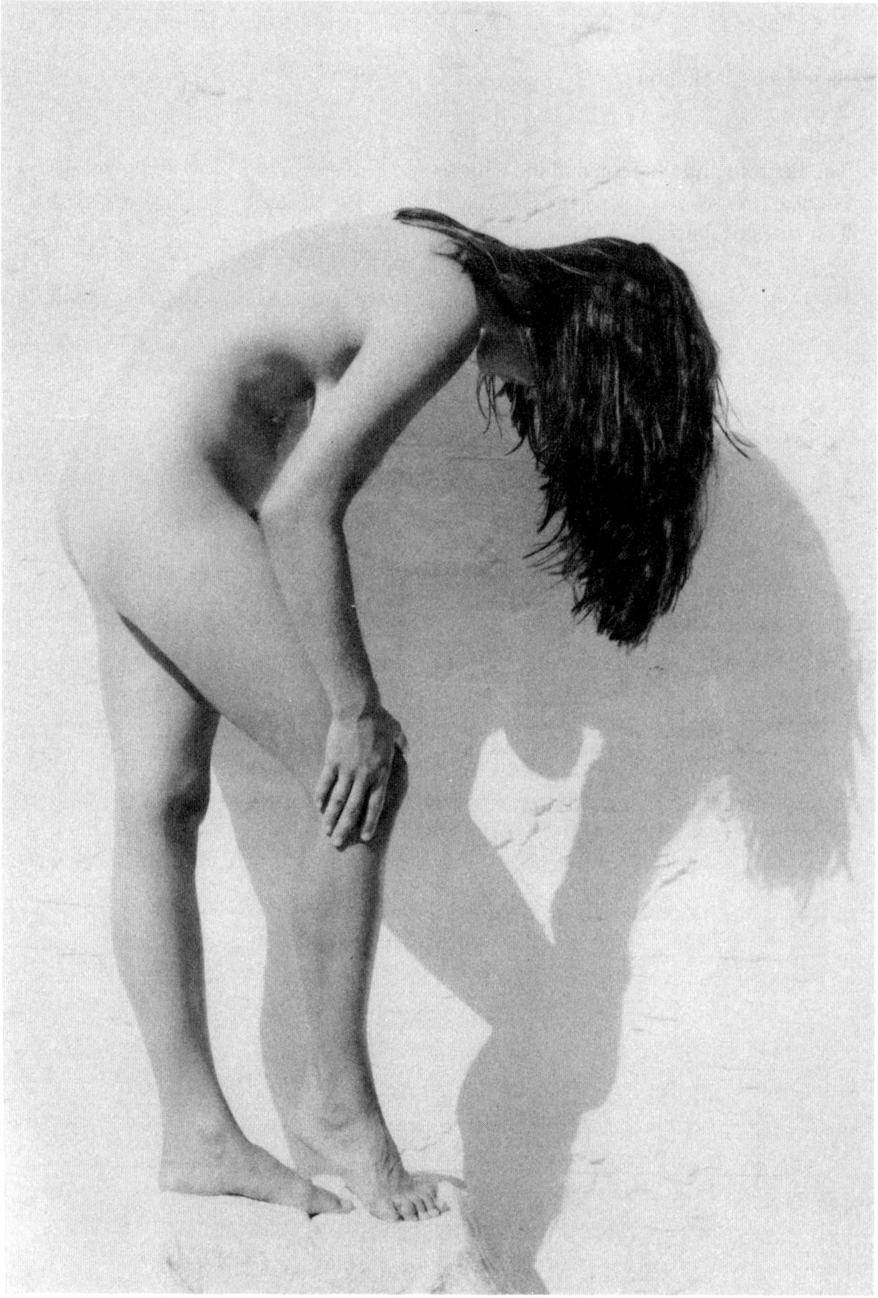

THE COW AND THE LYRE: AN INTRODUCTION

1. THE CICADA

In the 7th century BCE, on the prosperous island of Paros, lived an aristocrat named Telesicles, the same whose picture Pausanius saw in the Parthenon's Pinacotheke. According to the story carved on a stone in the Paros museum, one day Telesicles sent his son Archilochos to fetch a cow to market. On the way the boy met three lovely country lasses. In response to his teasing, for he was a lively lad, they charmed him, took his cow, and left him a lyre in exchange. Later the oracle at Delphi confirmed that the Muses had endowed him with song. He made songs of praise, of blame, of myth, of pleasure, of grief, of war, of seafaring, of women, and of song itself. Iambus, he said, was natural to him: "You have taken a cicada by the wing." Only blind Homer, from the previous century, was more renowned.

In Hellenistic times these kinds of stories were regularly attached to olden poets. Today we must do it for ourselves: give our cow, get our lyre.

2. THE PARIAN MUSES

I claim the Parian Muses - to whom, says Callimachos, Cretan Minos prayed - the way Yeats claimed spirits: prudent, he denied them.

I have lived on Paros since 1970. Consequently, most of my poems were written with wave-beat behind them, and in the afternoon when it is hot and the raucous crow sleeps, the cicada chirps our afternoon dreams. Girls' laughter, I remember, is both mocking and serious.

From the New York jazz of my youth, from Pindar's lines on the page that Hölderlin loved, from a line of Marvell and the forms of Herbert, from mad Pound and desperate Eliot, I started to build, in the Aegean surf, a Nymphaion, where Keats could say Minos' cadenced words.

3. LINKAGE

A poem expresses a precise condition of subjective awareness whose intensity induces the possibly true perception that it has coalesced with objective awareness, the way the four basic forces of physics coalesce when energy levels are sufficiently high. Poetry is a condition, that is to say, of unity at high energy.

But of what is the poet aware? Of the tragedy - which implies nobility - of the human predicament; of the comedy - which implies foolishness and even despicability - of human nature: of the interconnectedness of all things; of the frightening depth of evil in us all; of love and loneliness; of the inescapable fact of death and loss. Poetry, the most disturbing of the arts, is a stay - a foolhardy, noble stay - against inevitable loss and dissolution, whose method is to focus directly on loss and dissolution, and however inadvertently, to celebrate it. Its rapture of rhythm and diction, its precision of intuition, its fervid personal voice that would speak for us all, the linguistic voluptuousness of its despair: these make it a powerful and pleasurable tool for seeing the world and ourselves with unaverted eyes. Perhaps if I myself could link, like atoms in a new molecule of inestimable value, the scientific, the philosophical, and the poetic modes of perception, I would not suspect that such a linkage is the chemistry of Wisdom.

4. THE DOLPHIN AND THE TEMPLE

Whitman, who failed to exorcise the past, has become the past. When memories and emotions join their streams into a single river, when traditional forms are recreated so to render our own time with a full and even mimetic relationship with the past, when expressionism has been replaced by expressivity, perhaps a poem is genuine. The new poem is, then, a repository of primitive terrors, joys, and forms.

Consequently, I am suspicious of confessional poetry. A poet's life is in his work as a bird's life is in his, whose good news is in the way he sounds, in the insistent, cocky warble of his metres, rhymes, and metaphors. This good news proclaims, from the treetops of despair, the miracle of existence; his verses are personal in that they are meant to convert their writer more drastically than their readers, if they have any.

Most poets know these things very well. And there is an additional irony here. For this most serious and responsible of activities - the making of poems - depends on the frivolous and irresponsible. It is likely that a poet is not meditating on higher things while he works, but is playing with language and sound, with free association and planned dissociation, with personal griefs and grievous enmities, with elaborate conceits and tricks of rhetoric. He is hardly distinguishing between the empirical and the fantastical, or checking his beliefs against reality, or even bothering to steer clear of mere self-gratification. This is what we mean by the amorality of art, and is why Plato banned Homer from his scary Republic. The irony is that this haphazard and capricious process leads to that secret Republic whose archons are Homer, Dante, and Shakespeare. That poetry has vanished from the lives of most of us is a characteristic malaise of our time, an oecological disaster of the sensibility. Will the dolphin of the imagination continue to leap in such polluted seas?

Yes, poetry fuses failure with joy. It is an escape from reality that affirms reality, and that wants the vanishing world to participate in its escape.

Thus I leave moderation to others, and try to make a unity of ruins and springtime, in which the ruins once more become marble stones, become nature. To celebrate the return of her prodigal daughters Nature has laid out a profusion of flowers, and set us to build a Parthenon.

5. WOMAN, SONG, NATURE

I am not sure that it is a good thing to be as immediately impressionable as I am. Woman, singing poetry, and my natural surroundings keep me changing. As for women, I have my wife and I have my eyes. As for song, if I read a musical poem, by Sappho or Shelley or Baudelaire, I am fairly sure to write an imitation. As for my surroundings, sea and rock have meant to me what woods and running water meant to Wordsworth.

In the rough Hellenic landscape everything is very close. Even on the Greek mainland, here is the horned mountain and gentle hillock, here the valley, there a couple of white villages, yonder the sea and islands. It is as if an immense landscape had been modelled in a local god-sized museum for god-touched humans to contemplate with their limited purview. Is Greece unique in this succinct grandeur? What the ancient Greeks made was to elaborate a focus that had always been active.

The sea in Italy, where I go when I can, has a completely different aspect from that in Greece. In Italy, there are long straight coasts with few harbors; the sea is blank, uninviting, endless, a white space on a mediaeval map, leading nowhere. It is a dazzling wall to the imagination, a fading into nothingness. No wonder Odysseus was confused, directionless, once Athena's outraged tempest blew him west. In the Greek archipelago, there is always an island in sight, a suggestive shape on the horizon, a low mast, a chug-chug from an exhausted boat-motor, a couple of lazily arching dolphins - and so people, villages, the smell of earth and plants, sealanes, treacherous rocks and currents to be sure, temples, and tall tales. Mythology and history make the Hellenic pelagos rich, with its stern forms for the classical minded, its immemorial azure suggestiveness for the romantic. There is a reason why the words "Aegean" and "Ionian" are so much richer than "Adriatic" and "Tyrrhenian", though the salt air is equally bracing, equally inebriating. In Greece, "nymphs and Satyrs copulate in the foam", while in Italy the sea falls away, no stars constellating its zoneless expanse with the consolations of myth.

6. ICON

Michelangelo crowded his heaven with Greek bodies robbed of freedom, and Beethoven sobbed "O!" in the Gloria of his solemn mass. Michelangelo's fresco technique was the most conservative of his age, and Beethoven could hardly think without Haydn's sonata form.

So metre drives poetry. Though Whitman abandoned metred verse for versicles, Pound and Eliot, who end-stop their lines, still assume you hear it in your head. Poetry that depends on metre and yearns for a Renaissance Latin of aesthetic high culture is peculiarly American, for Americans are wolves of the wilderness. Abraham, who made his own idols in the wilderness, could never forget Ur.

I try to remember. Poesy is Greek for making, and icon for image. With Greek light and the English language, I have sought to reach that horizon where Helios and Hades touch, and then to look back at the world as though through an icon brightly: that is, to be really here. Then, in a song, starting with an imaginary "I", the verse that finds me may "lament the cow I have lost and praise the lyre I have found."

Ah, we can be more than we are. When Nike adjusts her sandal, you hardly notice her wings.

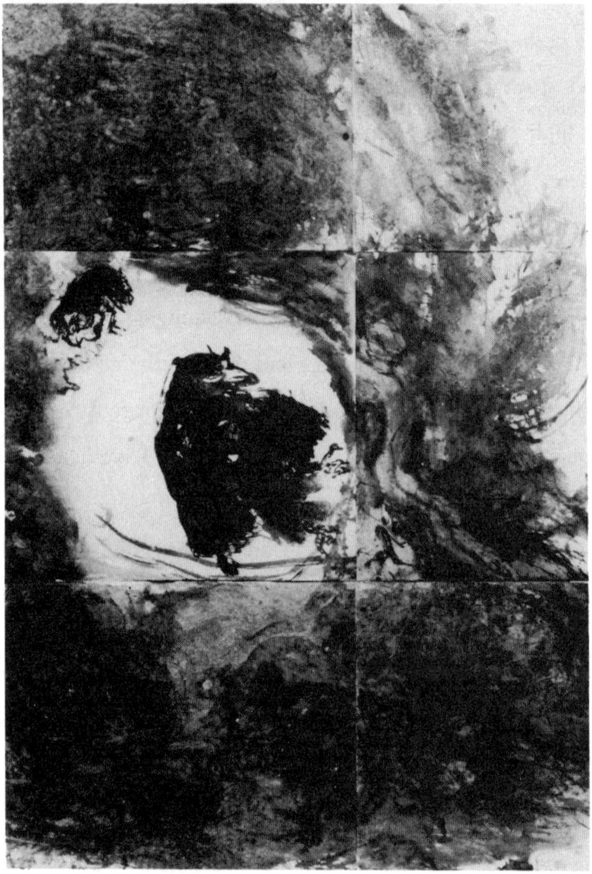

HARD LIGHT

1974-1983

Seek ever to stand in the hard Sophoclean light
And take your wounds from it gladly.

--Ezra Pound, "Ité"

FIRST SERIES: CONSTELLATION

Sure thou wilt joy by gaining me.
--George Herbert

CONSTELLATION

I

Often we watch, as the sea combs its own
Streaming grey hair, for the arrival
Of a single star's careful seaweed codes.

Because the perfect constellations
Contradict change as we move
Our tired eyes along the ecliptic
Unless we rearrange them for ourselves
Disregarding dead sanctities,
We relinquish expectation,
And recalling the voyages of our ancestors
Shift our eyes to the soft white
Of the evening's wavecrests.

Yet even subaqueously
The formal drama of the stars flowers
From the salt seed we may never find
Though we seek along every barbaric shore,
In every distant migration of swans and swallows,
Amid the discouraging mists and winds of the heart.

O my beloved
As light is bent by gravity
The constellated stillness of our love
Is moved by confusion's origin.

II

We farmed, once, these fields
For ten thousand years before the well went dry.
The clear water gave us our health,
As well as keeping our trees in flower.
But I have no skill for finding water,
And the water-diviners have started taking money
And are not so successful as before.

The malevolences of the shadows,
The goddesses with swollen hips,
The immortal ideas of the constellations,
The sanctities beyond blasphemy,
All disappeared long before
We ceased taking pleasure in the ritual.

And what but water can restore
The mystery to a dry well?

III

The whole of heaven is harmony and number
Stars shine as though through a flute's breathing-holes
Changing   it finds rest
The limbs of the gods were made to tremble

By the red of the poppy I swear
There are things in which mind also is

Yet do not ask me
I do not know what substance is
I do not know what virtue is
If I were better at solving puzzles
I would trust my thoughts and sensations

You wrap yourself in your silence
Hoarding a few fresh flowers
And the sun through the scarcely moving leaves
Faintly shows a bit of pale shadow
In which nor dark nor light is ascendent,
But the alternations of stone and star.

IV

Who will re-erect
The fallen walls the terraces on the hillsides
When even the houses stables shrines
Are devastated
And only bones have the whiteness of brine?

Each summer seems dryer
Than the last, fewer birds
Disturb the grating of the cicadas.
Figs pomegranates prickly-pears -
Food for crows.

It is getting more difficult to voice
The same questions incessantly:

Were our moments ever anxious with possibility?
How much is wind of the ancestral spectacle?
Was the Mayday wreath with its daisies
And garlic ever not withered and brown?

The wells have emptied into black space.

Where shall we journey?
Do we not know how far the stars are?

Untended stone gravemarkers
Black except glinting where chipped,
Broken terra-cotta lamps -
How did they glean grain from stone,
Extract rain from the stars?

V

When the silver Pleiades
Descend to the water like swans,
Submerge so as to appear
Mere wave-glitter
To fierce swashbuckling Orion,
Even then, toiling for wine and wheat,
We long for the wreathèd sea.

Prudent, we watch the writing
Of birds and the blessings
Of the sleek sun. With the Dog Star

We launch our swart ships
For fifty days after the sun sets west,
When the sea-breath can be compassed
And the sirocco not weaken men's resolve.
And that is the high life for a man,
Free of womanly snares,
Risking death amid the indifferent waves.

Even on land the salvagers eye us hopefully
Even as the depths turn toward us
Nestling the wind.

VI

We sailed so long one adventure
Seemed hardly distinct from the next;
Though you would gape at our hearthside tales
The exotic excites in small doses only.

But you get used to fatigue at the oars,
Grow indifferent as the waves to salt and spume,
Vague with an almost soothing homesickness.
And the sea, as you row, allures like a woman:
Rose at dawn, wineblue at noon, gold at dusk,
More of a drug than lotos-syrup.

As the grey shore fades
The rising squall is familiar enough.
Of course, with sharp winds and thunderheads gathering,

It is prudent to be afraid,
But we have got used to the fear.
As we row in rhythm, whelmed with sea-roar,
The waves' numb grief wills endurance.
We have eaten, and for now we are satisfied.

VII

To the sound of the double flute
I put forth my hand and beg
From the apple tree a fruit;
Having lost all my friends to the waves
Just you and I may eat.
As light bends round the earth
It mutes the wet well-stones.

When it rains we don't need wells. . .
With rainbow light we don't grow old. . .
A word you whisper to a snail
Outlasts a rainbow's resonance
And sparrows and honeybees reply
That your hair's best ornament
Is still fresh flowers.

VIII

In the lamplight the shadows
Bend like fingers along the whitewashed wall
In among the spider-guarded crevices
Across the bamboo and the battered window;

I see your arm, penumbra'd by the lamplight,
Move to turn down the flame;
The owl cries *kou kou vayia* from a cypress
While waves beat faintly on the beach below.

The seven virtuous senses -
Sight smell hearing touch taste
Thought and intuition -
Are the only trustworthy vanities
To yield profit without useless labor.

After the rains flooded the fields,
Made a shambles of the terracing,
Beat the blossoms from the almond boughs,
Though the crystal gleam of the rocks and leaves
Refreshed and rejuvenated us
We had no ambition for the heavy work,
Remembering the recent dead.

The voyages we had made,
The shipwrecks we had suffered,
The fear as much as the profit assailed us.
We took no comfort in astrology
Nor in the lapis cloak of the owl-eyed goddess
Which contradicts what little can be gainsaid.
The seven constellations in their sphere
Make it impossible to register fault
Unless what to commend is evident.

The clear sky is a burden
Only if you cannot uplift your palms.
Because we do not crave a false salvation
Your flesh shines with a starlike sheen,
The object of all the senses' concitation.

IX

Are the waves created suddenly
By the shifting of the continents
To continue moving rift by rift
With a wake of desolation?
Who can compass such forces and stay sane?
Nevertheless, the marked pattern helps us,
Even the terror of a ripple;
One windbent tree on a rock shore helps us;

The way you arrange your long lustrous hair
Helps us.

Tragedy, beloved, is a form of praise
For the foison of the earth
Which reclaims it savagely.
Have I sung offkey, are the birds offended?
Are the words terrible, or trivial?

In your far eyes the tumult of night
Slurs the throbbing of the stars.

Shall we call the sea bitter
When a thousand rainbows of spume
Distribute the morning sun as alms?

X

The sharp cry of the gull
Streaks the live rose of dawn.

You too heard the gull -
A cry that used to frighten us
When we sought fate in the tired stars
In the dreary sea even in the beating heart
Never penetrating the raiment
Calling a few tatters a drama of ourselves
Which would mow or arrange the flowers of confusion.
The very cry becomes a point of light
In a sky black as deep well water.
The icon of the seven saving senses
Even when it is a mere mirror
Is miraculous because it never changes its name
Nor regrets the wilting of the votive poppies
Nor the small hands that airily arranged them.

XI

Having heard the gull
Having held the shell
Having touched the flesh

The streaks of sunset turn you to face me
The swallows of dusk turn you
The streaming grey mirror of the sea turns you
The faint glow of the evening star turns you
Even the ancient creaking of the well-winch
Turns you and the light
In the sky in the backlit waves in the flowertops
In the gull's wingtip on the edge of cloud
The light in my reflecting eyes
Bends to you as you turn

The crescent moon turns in your direction
The emeralds of dusk on the waves trees hilltops
Are a corona for your golden hair

The curvature of space would be proved
Were I to avert my eyes -
Were I to step away
Flowers would obliterate the path.

XII

Poppies grow amid the asphodels.
Mountain sea and plain the light concords.
The glitter the curl the wind are rewards.
Waterbugs write in the deepest wells.

The words combed from the covert heart of praise
Change with the celerity of nightclouds

Concealing and revealing still stars.
No words of suffering attributed to
The trembling of eternity
Will compass what is plainly seen:
When stars shine in the seaswell
Permanence is a harbinger

For the single and unnamed
Constellation.

SEA STAR

I *Five Marine Pentastichs*

1

This early morning
the thin clouds seem to reach
into the still surface
of the sea -

even the fish are curious.

2

What did we lose that we can't remember
on the beach where no one goes?
Even the smooth pebbles you gathered
are dispersed -

even the shells.

3

A tiny fish in
the purple urchin
proves
the existence of the soul -

a handful of spines.

4

Iridescent silver fish a finger long
flicker, then turn colorless -
do you know where they've gone
or how they've become

invisible?

5

And yet the swarm
seemed to expand
hovering with the slight sea-motion:
little atoms of luminescence

in a galaxy of blue light.

II *Lesson*

In the mists of nebulae
are eyes of unbelief
beyond dejection,

amid the threaded colors
are richer blacks
that do not define anything -

a star's disgorged calligraphy
once committed to memory
always refers to a bird.

III *Like Your Days*

On clear mornings the caïques
vanish in the distant heat-haze,
some with sails, some with motors,
some with only oars.
Like your days they are different
every time.

That one leaving now
used to have a painted mermaid
holding her pointed breasts -
the hull has been repainted white;
a circle of caïques closes in
on a turning school of silver bream;
most of the hulls are white
but there are some blue, some flame-orange.

A bright green one joins them;
it is the one you like best.

A sudden meltemi catches them
as they draw in their nets.
pitching amid silent whitecaps:

again like a wind, again a moving sea.
Like your days they are different
every time.

When all the caiques are in
and safely out of sight,
though I speak of last year's mermaid,
it is only the color green
you care to remember.

IV *Sea Star*

The little Pleiades set
in the hushed water.

The Morning Star
whispers over Paros.

THE CYCLOPS TO ODYSSEUS

Wealth's the wise man's god,
The rest is talk and show.
The shores of the fishy sea
Mean not a thing to me.
Thunder I do not dread,
Nor the future that I cannot know.

My belly round with wine,
I make no sudden move,
And sleep after I eat
The most convenient meat
The sleep of the divine.
It is my own routines that I most love.

The earth grows grass for me
To fatten up my sheep.
I take my own advice
And make no sacrifice.
I wish great misery
On those who would make laws for me to keep.

I ask from no man
The hospitality
That I don't give to you.
The mouth is made to chew,

And I've a thrifty plan

To rid myself of prattling company.

METONYM

Blue dolphins follow the white caique
past the Two Towers
                    the black the red
bleak hills of Antiparos
                                        Strongylon deserted
                                        but for the ancient bones
                                        a place to gather spices

bow to Siphnos
          mountain crests like a line of music
seablue with the intensity of whitewash
no hint of turquoise
                                        and the sea
                              above the smile of the horizon
                                        the blue sea-shallows

Smiling the battered marble goddess lies
          in a field of bloody poppies

Blue dolphins in blue water
          inevitable gulls
ripples like tiny folds
          over the sea's breast

the broken engine amid the whisper of windlessness
and of dolphins reentering the wake

the cry of gulls in the wake of air

Cattle drink from the mossy trough
sarcophagus with bucrania
green surface of the water
The priest keeps behind the iconostasis
the altar with bucrania
for his private use

Stone mystery of whitewash
blue dome on the white chapel in the white village

Canst thou smile with a dolphin's smile
Or cast poppy seeds on the hill
Canst thou reach the whitewash's shadow
Or discern the moon in the whitewash's glow

in the village of Castro
chapels cluster like clover
and great flat stones scrupulously outlined
in whitewash

and a straight drop to the sea
caique motionless in the bay
gray-white rocks and
white flowers that were capers
lentisk   dittany   thorny-burnet
pollen   dust   pollen

and the far Parian hills flat
the delicacy the most austere
gray flat stones outlined in whitewash

the translucence of serenity
a clear life ensuing
and the blood pattern of poppies austere

swallows
with the wisdom
of rocks
25 kilometers from Castro to Paroikia
of a calm sea with dolphins between
rocks
with the wisdom
of swallows
mute and haphazard

The marble form in the flower field
goddess with a dolphin's smile
kore of the moon in noon light

The quiet field

there is no place that does not see thee
holding a bunch of poppies to thy breathing breasts
and the hot sun shining

RAVAGED BY BLUE

In anger the peregrine circled my head
as I fished by St. Spyridon's Rocks,
both of us ravaged by blue.
I waved my speargun at it as if
to threaten the sun itself, when
the sea's own silver fish arose
with its drop of blue sealight
and we both fell back in stillness.

SWIMMING

Swimming, you
are the horizon,
you are the
            silver line
but at noon
and the sharp sunrays
go straight up and down

blue and light

horizontal, yet
you can feel the sea
a curve,
and curved around you,
                        the center

I dive
beneath your nakedness

and see the seaweed
rising

WALL

A high wall of rubble
between two cut fields

From the other side
not a sound

Only your voice

faint as the moon
in the sky's pitiless blue

AFTER HSIA KUEI

The absolute changes
its weeds.
The fog is drawn
as with an inkbrush
where Spyridon's rocks
still emerge from the sea.
The water is calm and blue.
The chapel atop the rocks
is gray with lack of light.
Not one peregrine, not one cormorant,
disturbs the line of fog.
As in a Chinese seascape
it is too quiet to think
about anything at all.

ALBA

The dawn rises fresh and sweet; night dew
glows on the gray case
of my intellect; new shoots break through,
green and fuzzy with new buds (the wind
blows lightly from the west, and above
the clouds are petal-tinted rose and
cream; on the surface
of the sky these cloudwisps barely move
up to the horizon's silver blue).

I call such dew the tears of her eyes,
wide and weather-green,
yet my intellect knows no surprise
at such an improbable conceit;
for what else can I know, hope, expect
if my own pulse doesn't catch the beat
even and serene
of the sweet new style of intellect,
a dawn syntax of love's enterprise?

New shoots break through, and grown at once they
form a garden where
in solitude that lasts a long day
lovers move in gladed light and shade,
and what's wild is ordered by the eye
to a symmetry divinely made

which derives compare
from her perfection's bold modesty
as her night-attire is dropped away.

Her body shines smooth and flower-pale
to instruct the fruit
in true resemblances (a female
concern for natural nourishment:
in her thighs, hips, breasts, and flaxen hair
distribution's store is resident),
to be round and sweet
and reach full ripeness at the noon hour
when beauty's most intellectual.

Nature's artificiality
shows where the boughs pleach
and the leaves weave symmetrically
and the grass and flowers form a mat
that's soft with the light and fragrant-strewn,
so intellect may reformulate,
within her green reach
of all her garden, her living June:
thus the mat and leafy canopy.

For all the rich green is amorous,
and the varied song
of birds' calls, cicadas' susurrus,
leaves' slow rustle, beats in the very

pulse of our pleasure. Even at dusk
the secret flesh of rhyme (why bury
in dry dust the long
verdant noon?) will bloom with beauty's risk
and the dawn's dew hold all light for us.

FOLK SONG

A little fishing boat sets out
From the seaside, from the shore;
A little fishing boat sets out
From our pretty little Hydra
And it goes to look for sponges
From the seaside, from the shore.

Aboard are many fine young men
From the seaside, from the shore;
Aboard are many fine young men
Who go diving after sponges
And the pretty colored coral
From the seaside, from the shore.

All health and joy to you, young men,
And good fortune, and good luck;
All health and joy to you, young men,
May you bring us many sponges
And the pretty colored coral
From the seaside, from the shore.

EASY THE HOURS

Easy the hours. The stony land,
With all the edible generation of spring,
Is ambivalent with us.
And we, surely, are alone now.

So there is no comfort, no consolation,
No hope, no help,
Nothing to love for sure.

Easy the hours. The fabled sky
Arranges stars like notes for us to play.
We have never detoured our deaths
Which are not about to happen.

So where are we really then
To call our daily beach "Hellas"?
Even now, even us?

AT APHRODITE'S SPRING

Up at Aphrodite's spring
In the moist green dip between peaks
The blackglazed potsherds lie strewn
Among the stones and thistles;
Sprigs of maidenhair fern
Hang from the spring's walls.
Between daydreams I listen
To the crows, the sea, the wind,
At last to nothing at all,
Not even the goddess's
Footsteps, moist in the dry earth.

DESIRE

We sit at the seaside café,
My friend and I, with the other tourists,
And watch the twenty-year-olds
Clumsily display themselves.

Even the sunset, between Kea and Kythnos,
Glows, pretty and unexpected; we say little.

My eyes are for les jeunes filles
En fleurs, his for
The boys. If I miss a pretty girl
He points her out to me, and vice versa:
We know each other well.

Our desire is vague, general, untroubling
And enduring as our long friendship.
He's just left his longtime lover;
I'm still married, happily.
We order another ouzo; he's deciding.

The afterglow suffuses
The girls' bare, new-bought dresses.

THE GESTURE

Toward the pale horizon line
Past these islands, I gesture sadly
For the seagull out of sight
Merged in seasky azure; and now
A lonely mainsail rises slowly
Gleaming like an April cloud;
And to this island red with poppies
Comes the quiet of communion,
The odor of the hidden ocean.

TWILIGHT

Chinaberry leaves flutter in the twilight
About the terrace as I sip my raki;
The clouds that peak All Saints' Mountain
Are muted somber bronze;
The little waves in the quiet bay
Lap loudly in the accustomed silence;
In the thinning light I try
At your earnest request to write
A few connected lines of verse,
My mind fluttering aimlessly.

ELIZABETHAN SONNETS

I

A modern poet, am I right to write
A slew of sonnets to my lady's fame?
Have I the spark to fire me every night
To rhyme? I do: I have her living name.

Saying the word, I see her once again
(Though she is sleeping with an even breath
In the next room), and move my waiting pen
To make a sonnet "To Elizabeth".

Though it's unfashionable to call her Muse,
She's been thus generous for half my life;
Her form, face, and thought are my latest news:
Beloved Mistress, Donna, Lady, Wife,

These sonnets are a gratitude from me
To praise our fifteenth anniversary.

II

In spite of boyish thought and thoughtless wish,
Love taught my wordy clogged imagination
Of Woman and the courtesies of flesh,
Virtue and importunate expectation:

Eroticism leads lost life to love,
Even if it's but the external part,
Like noon flight to an island-dwelling dove
In seawinds which fetch o'er the common heart.

Zetetic for her loveliness's metre
Age has but quickened into poetry,
Bourned by manhood, I still when I greet her
Entreat her to our heightened appetency.

The beauty Love instructed me for life
Holds me within the rhyme, "Beloved Wife."

III

All through the cool unfurling morning hours
My mistress moves with perfect wifely grace
About her toilette and her early chores,
A pearly dewlike poise upon her face.

In summer while the weather does not rain
And the sky even at dawn is hugely blue,
She waters her green garden from a can
More fragrantly than a passing nymph could do.

When she espies me coming from the well,
She turns to me the seadrops of her eyes
And offers me the flower of her smile
Spontaneously, as if in surprise.

And nonchalantly asks from me a kiss
And all the morning moves now unamiss.

IV

Who's she that cometh so that all may see?
Who maketh scintillant the brilliant air?
Who bringeth Love as she comes gracefully
That none can speak, but sigh that she is there?

Ah, as she glanceth round, let Love declare
(For I could ne'er describe it) how that she
Doth seem a lady of much modesty
That by her all but seemeth wrath and care.

Her pleasingness is undescribable
Since gentle virtues all to her do bend
And beauty for its goddess showeth her;

Our minds have ne'er been so upraised before
Nor can such perfect grace to us descend
That we can ever know her to the full.

--CAVALCANTI

V

My lady is so gentle and so wise
That when she greeteth men their every voice
Doth tremble and go still, and gazing eyes
Avert themselves secretly to rejoice.

She passeth, hearing naught but words of praise,
Attired most kindly with humility;
It seemeth she hath come among our days
To show a miracle that's heavenly.

She showeth pleasing fair to look upon
That through the eyes the heart is made more sweet
Which none can comprehend to her unknown:

It seemeth from her beauteous face doth fly
A spirit full of love that goes to greet
The soul to say to it these words: "O sigh."

--DANTE

VI

Splendid star of dawn, donna d'amore,
You irradiate my heart erotically
That I recall our first hesitant foray
Into love's dawn and its rich lambency.

Let that sweet hour return and all its joy
Of dalliance, when I first said to you,
"Though I am yet an inexperienced boy,
The sudden love that is between us two

"Will not prove false for anything that is,
And will not leave me when I am a man
But make me one." From our first helpless kiss,

We've never lost the radiance of that dawn,

Nor ever let that early light disperse,
But gathered it like rhyme-words in a verse.

VII

"In form a cloud all smoke departs its fire
"With bearing grave, and wafting ever higher
"Despoils itself till at its uppermost
"It's all transformed and so resolved to naught.

"What then would it be like to penetrate
"Into the permanence of her perfection?
"When I imagine past my power of thought,
"When to my peril her face I contemplate,
"My eye and sense subside into subjection
"And in her image I am wholly lost."

Englished out of Maurice Scève, this dizain
Has given me a needful metaphor
And feeling so that I may rhyme once more
The meanings she allows into my ken.

VIII

How richly yellow I'd like to descend
Drop by drop as a sweet golden rain,
When sleep glides o'er her eyes at evening's end,
Into my lady's breast, and there remain.

And I should like to be transformed into
A milkwhite bull to seize her when she goes
In April 'mid the newgreen grasses' dew,
A flower who a thousand flowers knows.

And I should like - such is my heart's desire -
To be Narcissus so were she the pool,
And plunge myself in coolness through the night;

And more: to take the canker from delight,
May it unfold eternally beautiful,
And day's dawn ne'er ignite with different fire.

--RONSARD

IX

Here murmur all the spindrifts of the waves,
Here tremble all white blossoms and green leaves
And spiceplants in the gentle morning breeze,
And o'er the newgreen branches of the trees
Enamored and alighting birds beguile
The lazy east into a roselipt smile,
So that the sloe-eyed dawn shows suddenly
Mirrored in the island's windward sea,
And as the spacious lightening sky grows wide
The sweet mild dew empearls the countryside
And gilds each outcrop and each mountain height.

O warming dawn, eager and flower-bright!
The messenger breeze (thou art her counterpart)
Revives (O waiting love!) the parchèd heart.

--TASSO

X

I rushed headlong, thrust by romance and lust,
Into a lasting love and interest
And female Wisdom when I ceased to trust
The ephebe's laws my mind ordained as best.

An ephebe's laws? That's pure tomfoolery
One heartache is sufficient to disparage:
A real woman offered herself to me
And not a neat prospectus of a marriage.

That I shrugged off the fake antitheses
Of love or freedom, to wander or to wed,
Lets me now praise the loving expertise
She's since acquired in garden and in bed.

And praise the intuitions of a boy
Who chose long life in a single moment's joy.

XI

Who says that he must shed his wedded wife
To enrich himself with hued variety,
To lead a brighter more faceted life

Than he could live entombed by family,

Is right: a ready change is beneficial
To the senses and the mind; a grown man's
Virility is wildly unofficial
And not to be hemmed-in by wedding bands.

Thus restless, I could never love the same
Woman for a lifetime: And I do not,
When I make verse to her unchanging name,
Blot my flowing pen in just one spot.

The mistress that my self still seeks to know
Subsumes the girl gained fifteen years ago.

XII

When seeking inspiration I peruse
Old sonnets praising lovely mistresses,
Entreating them and claiming them for Muse,
Denying them all daily blemishes,

I wonder to myself, as I admire,
If beauty must be gazed at from afar,
Or through a mist or suddenly kindled fire,
As unattainable as any star.

My mistress had great beauty in her youth
And still blooms with a beauty beyond most;

I praise it with great pleasure and in truth
As both an introspection and a boast.

But my sonnet's livelihood chiefly depends
On qualities of hers that have no ends.

XIII

Green pebbles rounded by the light-filled sea,
White shells that gleam in shallows and on shore,
A finch that sings in our mimosa tree,
Our kitten waiting by the curtained door,

Green herbs and flowers wet in earthen pots,
A flower-scroll on the rough whitewashed wall,
A morning of caresses and love-thoughts,
A rhyme well-worked and subtly passional,

A clavichord that mutes a summer night
With courtly dances and their divagations,
A photograph that's eloquent with light
On solid rock or seavague undulations:

When my verses are restless and obscure
I name what she loves to effect a cure.

XIV

Sometimes past midnight I reach out to touch
Thy sleeping cheek, and listen to thy breath

To allay the gnawing worm of self-reproach
By whispering a word, "Elizabeth":

And I admit my deepest desperations
I'd shrug my shoulders at when we're awake
Because of dumb masculine imperfections
In silences I cannot yet forsake.

How near exhaustion is the heedful heart
When like a landbird carelessly off course
O'er ocean wastes despondently apart
It seeks wind-current to conserve its force.

But I am never long dispirited
When thou art lying next to me in bed.

XVI

I made these sonnets as a monument
To fifteen years of marriage that we share;
If our first lusting was coincident
And youthful, our first loving kiss was rare

And permanent, and rare to have increased
Despite the nigglings of unloving time;
And even lust's first burning has not ceased
But with learned expertise become sublime.

No, not a monument nor a gilt support -

What need have living things for such as these? -
Nor rhetoric to comfort or exhort:
This offering is merely meant to please.

I praise my future, Elizabeth, if you
Are what my zodiac is pointing to.

THESSALONICA

I bought two crimson roses in
The old hammam (the brightest reds
In this gray town) so that you might
Combat abed the winter's germs;
I went out to see the sights
Alone; fifty drachmas each,
They slowly opened for a week.
Most of the famous Byzantine
Churches were barred by scaffolding
Or closed because of the recent earthquake.
I went to Hagia Sophia twice
(The dome was boarded over) and
The second time a silent light
In the empty church lit up
With somber gleams the gold field of
The ancient polished tesserae
Of the apse's dull empyrean
On which a distant maid reposed
With her child; and I came back
To tell you how the picture spread
Its perfect petals for my council:
The deep elapses of my heart
Are moisture for a cut red rose.

SONNET: WHY I AM UNHANGED

If you're in love, but can't raise any cash,
You'd better build a gallows and go hang
Or else your gut aches with a twisting pang
Worse than the Devil's after his long crash.
Now for my sins I earned this punishment:
The god of love now hangs out in myself
To bug me with a hassling lack of pelf,
With no hand-outs from pals more affluent.

So why not hang myself with my own hand?
Because I have a last-ditch shred of hope:
My old man is a doddering moneybags,
And when he goes I'll score a hundred grand
(He'll kick the bucket soon or I'm a dope);
Till then God keeps him whole and me in rags.

--CECCO ANGIOLIERI

DONNA GENOVESE

You brought me a bit of seaweed
In your hair, and a smell of wind,
That has come from afar and arrives heavy
With ardor, was in your bronzed body:
 - Oh the divine
Simplicity of your agile form -
Not love or spasm, a phantom,
A shadow of necessity which wanders
Serene and ineluctable through the soul
And dissolves it in joy, in serene incantation
So the sirocco can carry it away
Through the infinite.
How small the world is and light in your hands!

--DINO CAMPANA

SNOW ON MT. PARNES

Fat wet flakes of snow
fall past the streaky window
of the hospital room
where I lie in pain
with a broken hip;
this is the most snow
the city's seen in years.
Leaning on my elbows
unable to turn or sit
I can see the ridge
of Mt. Parnes (where
iron knives were offered
on ashen altars) turn
unaccustomed white.
Everyone is complaining
at the difficult snow;
my next-bed neighbor who
shot off his foot while hunting
and crawled on elbows for
three hours to a road
warns his pretty wife
of high heels on ice;
visitors whose tulips
gleam on the windowsill
can't get cabs. The huge
cypresses before

the nurses' dorm (I can
only see the tops)
collect snow until
the rising wind knocks it
off in sudden gusts.
since this is my first
queasy brush with frail
mortality I don't
know what to make of it;
a kid was brought in dead
just yesterday - we heard
his mother's screams even
here on the fifth floor.
The snow keeps falling through
the evening blacks and night
so that next morning all
the mountain has gone ghostly
through dawn's frosted pane.

SECOND SERIES: PAROS CALENDAR

Stood on edge mid wave and wind.
--Archilochos

A JANUARY HOUR

Despite dawn glow it's easy not to see
How damp day lengthens looping like a hawk
About the greening hills and fields that hide
The wet inchoate year; I slow my stride
And find a place to pick
My way (I'm early for Epiphany)
Through northwind-stunted pines amid which lie
Empty sarcophagi
To the gullied path that edges the gray sea
Still waiting restless for the ritual
To burst with white the chambered magus-star
With all its colors of the waiting year.

A seagull crouches on a crumbling wall;
For birth or death, I think, and stare afar
As frightened he flies off, then circles back
To nearly the same spot, and in the sky
His folded wings appear and disappear
Amid clear patches clouding with his cry;
The ancient churchbells chime
Me once more into time
And roused I hurry to the crowded dock
In time to see old Papa Petros toss
Aloft a newly purchased golden cross:
Twelve greedy boys plunge through the freezing sea.

FEBRUARY SONNETS

I

Yeats thought, who pray in the Chapel of the Well
Or tree of nature's ripe abundance are
Content, who in the Chapel of the Star
Must mourn for paradise in an earthly hell.

Thus I muse on the anguish I foretell
In scanned horizons glowering from afar
To mock the foison of the Calendar
Or scorn the volutes of a wellsnail's shell.

When I pull water from our well, I pray
(Though I'm a wholly unreligious man
Too indolent for the rigors of belief)
For rain to soothe the gardens of my grief.

Does not Venus' Star ripen into day
On Paros where my sea-changed thought began?

II

We sip our morning coffee on the roof
Where the sun strikes first from over the hill;
It seems that we can hardly have enough
Of February sun on days so still.

For our new white kitten I throw a stone;
He plunges after it through the field's wet green;
The other two cats, agèd now, look on
With pleased disinterest, sunwarmed and serene.

The light of morning sparkles on the sea
Transparent in the utter lack of wind;
A greenfinch sings within the cypress-tree;
A kestrel hovers high and disciplined.

We look and sip and think nothing at all:
Such simple pleasure must be mystical.

III

In a blue terry robe she lounges about
The morning, straightening my studio,
The bedroom, and the kitchen, searching out
Snails from spices potted in a row.

The sun with a yellow yawn has risen late
And lounges in the pearly cloudstreaked east
To see the dewy morning dissipate
In winter weakness, wry, graceful, and triste.

The gloomy images I fabricate
To embue the fields and sea with suffering
Are flimsy to what I would now create
Were sun and she not so bewildering.

Such mysteries I do not need to probe:
She's naked underneath her morning robe.

IV

Heating water on the stove to take
A bath now that the winter sun's come out
And windlessness has left the bay a lake
On which white seagulls amorously shout,

We repent complaining that we've turned too old
To live comfortless as ten years ago,
And grumbling at the wind and damp and cold
And shivering boredom's tuneless tremolo.

Now that we've removed our dirty winter clothes
And pour the heated water on our heads
Your body's turning once again betroths
My flesh to yours:
                    Ours is the best of beds
(I think to see your thighs and breasts and cheeks)
When we have not been naked for two weeks.

V

Be wise, my sorrow, on this dreary day;
Be tranquil, though the sky rolls with unease,
The day brims boatless in its leaden gray,
The northwind rants; be simple in thy peace.

Beloved, take my hand and turn with me
To greet the evening fretless, in accord,
Impervious to threats of sky and sea,
Whose tolls exceed what we ought to afford.

For soon the darkening sun will touch again
To color Siphnos' cliffs a deep carnation,
And we shall hear the sweet night slowly train
In shimmering silence her long constellation.

O lie by me and grace me with thy gaze
That I may gem the sorrowful with praise.

VI

A sudden cloud-rift in the west as I
Go out to take a leak shows at my back
The evening star bright in the twilit sky
Not very far above the sea's grayblack.

What dull attire the temptress wears tonight,
Which parted shows her avid to embrace
A lover not indifferent to the sight
Before she sinks to a more secret place.

Into the closing clouds at last she goes
Through the low twilight's horizontal green;
In the black field I button up my clothes;
The sea and sky now share the same dull sheen.

The night goes black; there's not a star in view,
And shivering I go inside to you.

VII

We hang a blanket over the leaky casement
And huddled in bed watch it ripple and huff
With the sharp Vorias' darkening displacement
In a winter room that's never warm enough.

Unless I light our dwindling olive boughs
Cut from my neighbor's fall prunings and then
When the hissing of the fire makes us drowse
We can pretend that we are warm again.

We wait for day to counter with a Garbis
That pours its golden pitcher of warm rain
On all the archipelago of Greece
On wildflowers and fields of ripening grain.

We mock the winter's rage - two aging lovers -
By loving daylong underneath the covers.

VIII

A freezing wind is swirling on the sea
Stippled with drizzle; we had hoped today
To tend the garden, ragged and windblown;
We go back in, our mood put in reverse.

But sorrow's a unique nobility
Which neither hell nor earth can gnaw away,
Which must impose to braid the mystic crown
On every time and every universe.

And all of Paros' ancient treasury
Beneath the fields and shimmering sea-sway
And in the lime of Paroikia town
Contributes to the making of a verse

Which then becomes the fuel for our hearth:
We light the stove and count the day of worth.

IX

In the cold kitchen I wait for the water to boil,
And hear the northwind ridicule my plight;
The February sun will not get bright,
No southern rain will drench the island's soil.

Sipping my cup, I hear the stormwind roil
The bay; no fishing boats went out last night.
Awake, I go into my room to write:
What else to do but this accustomed toil?

My wife's at work, so I don't light the stove,
Not having wood enough should such cold weather
Last all month. Luckily a friend comes by;
We drink a pot of strong coffee together.

Alone again, I give it another try,
And scribble what I wasn't thinking of.

X

Anemones, pink campion, and rock-rose
Bloom on the hills where nothing useful grows;
And naked on its little curving stem
Shines the milkwhite star-of-Bethlehem;
Amid spiked thyme-thickets in the winy-blue
Grape-hyacinth, its upper buds furled tight,
Its lower stained with purple of night-dew
Is many breasted Artemis's emblem;
Behind wind-supple barriers of bamboo
Almond blossoms, all shivery and white,
Cling to their leafless boughs in the contrary
Northwind; in the ploughed wheatfields wild-clary,
Calendula, and sweet narcissus invite
A spring fertility to February.

XI

The morning gleams with tiny white snails
Like shell sailboats with storm-retracted sails
On the flowerpots and wet flattened grasses,
On the wood front door and the well's two pails.

The morning mist spins off its pearl distaff
Spidery threads on waves and wet seacliff
And drops a drowsiness on our first kisses

Before we let the dampness make us stiff.

Pecking at some frozen flakes of bread,
Undaunted by the northwind's butting head,
White wagtails rattle the cats' empty plate.

Since it's too cold and damp to leave the bed
We lie and love until the morning's late
And let our daily exigencies wait.

XII

The sky is cloudy and the air is chill;
The sea is turbid charcoal, frothed with white;
The wind's relentless on the terraced hill,
And bends the new wheat green in winter light.

Your pots of mint and parsley are protected
Behind a wind-fence of four-foot bamboo
Where black carpenter bees doze unsuspected;
An early calla shields itself there too.

You shake our blankets - no work in the wind,
Then plant spring seeds in fresh-dug soil I've brought;
Your bound-up hair comes suddenly unpinned;
I put my arms around you, in my thought

All the unavoidably imagery of
The front porch view and ordinary love.

XIII

While she's at work, I put off every chore,
To choose a favorite anthology,
Stuff up the crack under the kitchen door,
And warm myself with lyric poetry.

As always I read self-indulgently
The poems that I have often read before,
And know almost by heart. I brew some tea
And light myself a very rare cigar.

I say a couple of Keats' throbbing odes
And Spenser's fertile Epithalamion,
A Song of Experience, then move along
To try myself on less expected words -

Too late, and now my concentration's gone,
I fix our lunch, my heart flooded with song.

XIV

Protagoras said, "Man's the measure of
All things", which is to speculate that we,
Since ignorant of gods and of god's love,
Must of ourselves make our philosophy.

In the little church of Saint Demetrios,
Near where our housepath intersects the road,
The oil-lamp casts its light on a fresh red rose -

What living saint dare shoulder such a load?
Many women out this afternoon
Shrilly to gather dandelion greens
Pause inside to light a candle, and soon
The dark interior's ablaze.
He means
That what we know is a sufficient burden:
We cut the rose this morning from our garden.

XV

Well fortified with ouzo, I go down
To the beach below to take my yearly winter
Swim; the sun seems weaker and less warm,
The horizon hazy, the day windier.

The sand is littered with the torn detritus
Of the season's windstorms: stones, fragments of shell,
Blue plastic, seaweed; in the shallows an octopus
Holds eerily still as if in uncracked crystal.

A returning fishing-boat makes wavelets which
Reach to the trembling whiteness of my toes -
It's numbing. I back up onto the beach,
Swig from the bottle, and remove my clothes.

I plunge in, and suddenly sober, foolishly nude,
Thrash until I know I've been renewed.

XVI

Some sun shines through the thinning morning haze
As we take our dirty laundry to the well -
A chore postponed these freezing winter days.
Our kitten watches by an asphodel
Sprouting from the terrace's back wall.
I pull the water; she rinses with rubber gloves
Though the well doesn't seem cold at all.
The sea is calm, the azure hardly moves.
Finished, she sees a flower that she loves;
The kitten follows. (My head throbs with a rhyme:
The stillness of this leap year somehow proves
The yearly harmlessness of counted time.)
Returning to the well, smiling and happy,
She shows to me the spring's first bloodred poppy

MARCH SIROCCO

This wind could rip the house out by its roots
And fling its stones to fields where they were gathered;
New swallows huddle in its muddy eaves;
The garden is a mess; the citrus gripes
Its swirling blossoms; gray common gulls wait dully
In the wrecked olive orchard; the horizon grips
Sea-currents with its claw; the wheat's green shoots
Are hay; the slashed green canebrake rows shrilly
Groan from age; our windowpanes look weathered;
We hear the door assaulted and we cough
As southern salt pocks whitewashed walls in heaves;
By dawn the wind has choked itself with chaff.

APRIL WILDFLOWERS

Every morning as I go
down the hundred yards of the
housepath for the milk I count
how many different kinds of
wildflowers I see. Below

the path are terraces of
wheat turning from green to gold
and then is an orchard of
flowering lemon trees (though
there are still many lemons)

which seem to lean into the
sea which on windless days shows
the changing colors of sand
seaweed and rock in shallows
and then in dawn clarity

Syros, Seriphos, Siphnos,
which by noon will have faded.
On the way down I pass the
goat with her three kids (two will
go at Easter in two weeks)

and the chickens. Sometimes I
have to kick the rooster who

likes to fight in the morning.
My cat always goes with me
but waits at the chicken house.

This morning (I just put up
the milk to boil) I counted
twenty seven different kinds
the most profuse of which are
poppies (bloodred in the wheat),

asphodels, lavender-flushed
sage, and chamomile. I saw
the first iris open and
a rare purple poppy and
also the first creeper of

pale convolvulus which stays
all summer long. There were a
lot of butterflies and bees
in the sage and thyme flowers
and finches chirping in the

mastic tree, and gulls, and crows.
I'm so lazy I never
plant anything but my wife
does. In summer I make three
trips to the well every dusk

to keep her garden herbs and
flowers healthy but it is
still spring and so I only
have to go once a day as
there is plenty of night dew

and the chance of rain. There are
few summer wildflowers. My
wife also does beautiful
flower arrangements (the one
I liked best was just with the

crimson poppies set off by
the delicate sprays of white
lacy tordyllium). For
some reason she never wants
to use the yellow insect

orchids although they keep quite
well. Well, I must stop writing
this poem before the milk
boils over. But let me give
a moral in which I pat

myself on the back. Every-
body loves spring wildflowers
but not everybody takes

the care to regard them when
going for the morning milk.

MAY SUNLIGHT

I

How disparate is the midday sun
Motionless in waves of noon
(Thetic light unlike the moon

Which is a sea of beating waves
Sparkling with phosphorescent lives
Of stars, an earth of marble graves),

And our naked bodies on the sand
Uncooled by the faintest wind
Are no sunstruck Bacchic band

Although erotic in their spread.
The sun, we're sure to say, is good:
We praise it for our private food,

For the most high reality,
And for the gods of poetry:
Sovereign sun, eternal eye,

Most pure, most metaphysical,
Most distant, most ungazable,
Make imagination fill

The brine pits of our hearts with light
To gleam with sealight through the night,
Make what is real be also right.

II

The seascape is imaginative;
Too still for a rising second wave,
The blue ideas that we believe

Are seaformed as a murex shell
Gleaming in a seafloor dell
(We need not dive down deep to tell

Its spiny quaint white-whorled shape
Focuses the whole seascape
With its glintings from the deep

Our breath would barely reach but we
Might finger cold reality -
Whose locus is a moveless buoy -

With numbing hands), or as the cry
Of seagulls writing in the sky
Suggestions for a poetry,

Wings widesplayed for the noon sun
Or folded for the midnight moon
(Sunlight and moonlight shine as one

Single cry). Thus we say,
Floating on the film of day,
Such optimism is of May.

III

The whole month's wind moves in the sea
And stills it, so that it may be
The one wave of a poetry

That inevitably comes
With all its daylight of two dreams
(What is and what we'd make), two forms

Of real time, a noon Maytime
Smelling of thistle-flowers and thyme
And of the sea sparked with seabream

And the ripe wheat of summer's graves.
Swallows nesting in the eaves
Of seacliffs execute their dives

And flying by us do not land
Where we are lying on the sand
Grainy in the lack of wind;

A merest wisp of mare's-tail cloud
A seablue white drifts overhead.
Every foolish word we said

Was for the love of rhyme made wise:

In the lidless sun's just purities

We stretch ourselves and shut our eyes.

JUNE SOLSTICE DIPTYCH

In June the days seem impossibly long, and we wake up early to enjoy the cool colors of daybreak in sea and sky, and to do chores in the cool of morning. Dawn is the only time we can see the other nearby Cyclades - from our porch, Antiparos, Siphnos, Seriphos, Kythnos, Kea (a thin gray pencil line), Syros, Tenos, and between the hills of Hagios Phokas, Mykonos - since they entirely vanish in midday heathaze.

On the sea bob a dozen little fishing barques, and noisy groups of gulls on bay and offshore searocks.

Our house has four rooms, and is entirely built of stones from the fields. One room is for storage: one a bedroom; one for books, desk, piano, and clavichord; one (down a few steps, with a separate entrance) the kitchen. The house sits on a terraced hill (about a twenty-minute walk from Paroikia village) over the northfacing bay of Souvlia. All around are wheat and barley fields, some already harvested and some with the three-foot high stalks sunburnt gold. In the harvested fields, goats, cows, sheep, and donkeys, all hobbled, glean.

On either side of the house are squat broad-leaved fig trees with purple fruit in which wasps lay their eggs; also a straight cypress tree, a stunted almond, and a twelve-foot mimosa we planted ten years ago.

The house's rough walls undulate with whitewash; the floor is cement; the ceilings (from inside) beams and bamboo. The doors are rather low and we must stoop. The whitewash has been applied yearly for the house's whole 150 years, and this has rounded and softened all edges. There are some smooth-hewn marble blocks built into the walls, taken from the Pytheion which used to crown the top of the hill, and a marble grave-stele serves as a gatepost.

The porch is paved with flat flagstones between which weeds grow; part of it is covered over from midmorning shade. A great greenleafed chinaberry shades our pots of herbs (basil, mint, parsley, rosemary, chives, marjoram, dill), and flowers. The geraniums along the path, which require little precious water, are in full flower. Our little garden, in which we raise spinach, onions, and garlic, is dry for the summer except for a few tomatoes - too much sun and not enough water.

The house has two stone-lined wells, neither copious - one in the field overhead, and one adjacent with deep cold water. We have no running water, and in winter, bathing, now a pleasure, is quite difficult. We also have no electricity, and read by kerosene lamps, which shed a lovely soft flickering light. I usually go to the well in the cool of the evening, since it is better to water the garden when the sun is down. To wash the salt off after a swim, we usually just throw a freshly drawn bucket of water over ourselves, which makes us shudder.

The day is windless with just a hint of a seabreeze from the west - the Greek for this still Zephyros. The bay is still and limpid and so the underwater colors and configurations are unusually clear: sandribs, rocks, seaweed beds. I used to spearfish here years ago but now must seek out more remote spots, though there are still plenty of octopus. In the middle of the day the sunlight is so bright on the water, gleaming in silver points, that it is hard to gaze at steadily: the fish sleep; the fishing boats are all in. We also doze in the afternoon to the clamor of cicadas and sunlight outside the cavelike room, cool within its thick walls.

From the porch we can see the sun set just to the west of Syros; tomorrow it will start back until it touches, in December, the cliffs of Antiparos. The sunsets in June are not gaudy, except when there is a rare wisp of cloud to catch the colors, but we can see the sun turn red and flatten and sink into the sea, and watch the afternoon deepen into evening along a curved seahorizon of almost 180 degrees.

The nights are warm and we sit out late, when the porch fills with the odor of the honeysuckle climbing out of the old whitewashed cistern, and the spiders spin webs across the housepath, and moths whir by the lamps. We watch the planets and stars, and the crescent moon, no longer faint in the afternoon, set in a silver stripe in the black sea.

All the radiance of Paros has returned to the sun.

*

The basil and mint and marjoram
which she tends every day
with water from the well
one day unexpectedly
envelop you entirely
in the soft shock of their fragrance.

You sit on the marble bench
of stone from the Pytheion
(which glistens still in the whitewash,
the Slayer blanched Ionic),
and in one suspiration

you are empty as a seashell -
yet you see the sun shine
on the northfacing bay
and on the bleak hillside
with its wild thyme and sage
tended only by goats -
but cannot see if your eyes
are giving off the light,
which seems to move about you
as if underwater,
until she tells you so.

As she turns from her plants
to look out over the sea
lifting her breasts so that
they appear whiter and smaller,
the sudden shock of joy,
which if your eyes could see it
would frighten you forever,
ripples through the seafoam
of your hair and beard
with an absence of sensation
that is sensation itself.

And all the way from here
through the still baywater
your eyes can clearly see
signs on the ribbed sand

made when a Homeric bird
walked along the seafloor
with white celestial thoughts.
And as she turns to you
with her watering can,
and turns her breasts in their
open white shirt to you,
the legibility
of iridescent growth
in sun and sky and sea
is of all the garden's joy,
and of perfect various light
of ray and wave and leaf,
and of flat paving stones,
and of the ancient marble
where you sit thus struck.

So you say nothing and watch
the sea and sky, the flowers
and bees and butterflies,
so you say nothing to
become something else,
and blow to imitate
the wind, and the thin
woven veils open
one color at a time,

and the first bright shoots
of all your breathing moments
rustle with their blossoms,

and the white honeycomb cell
like a sunlit dewdrop
opens within so you
can speak the miracle
of the furthest sun
to all the days of Paros.

JULY NIGHT

Unable to sleep in the July night
I stroll down the dark housepath
Taking a stick to clear my way
Of a thousand spider webs;
Overhead a huge moth beats
Its wings and I look up to see
Each single star in the Milky Way
Shining with a single courage.

AUGUST

As gulls move the light
From one searock to another

The ghost of yesterday's fish
Again evades
The shiny hooks

SEPTEMBER

I

The last spring rain fell four hot months ago
And yet the mountain - its stones and purple thyme,
Its ants and crows and lizards, all hard and dry -
Still sends its cold streams to our deep well
Subterraneously; and blue aglow
With noon sunlight is the extreme sky
In which a raving seagull starts to climb
Until it seems a still sunlit shell.

Dry dust weighs down the silver olive trees,
Their ancient roots within the earth's pores;
Cicadas count the summer's even beat
Within the creaking of a bamboo row;
Slow and amiable the dusted bees
Buzz within the syllables of heat;
The sunlight in its stream rushes and pours
Its gold oil on the archipelago.

II

You lie beside me on the beach, your toes
Reaching to the moveless edge of sea,
Naked to the pitiless sun, a few
Drops of white seasalt between your breasts;
Limpets lie along the rocks in rows;
Waves from a boat approach your knees and you

Pull up your legs, and turn your hips to me,
And turn your glance from the sudden white wavecrests.

We swim, then fall asleep in the hot sun;
Awakened by the strange smell of rain
In the new arisen wind, we see a cloud
Floating over Siphnos, its udders shuddering
To grayblack tips; the sudden gooseflesh on
Your skin together with the shrimps that crowd
Your toes send you to swim before the rain
And all the island's roosters start to sing.

III

Amid the desiccated seaweed and sand
Opens the bell-crowned white seadaffodil;
The seasquill points its white flower-rows;
They drink the sharp sunrays like spring rain
As if you tended them with your own hand
In plots so dry that nothing ever grows;
No morning dew yet glistens on the hill
And the ground stays hard until it rains again.

The naked flesh of summer, burnt bone white,
By salt, and tremors of the heart's age,
And the birds who peck the thistle's dried seeds,
And pale medusae, and the sun's sweat,
And huge Scorpius rising in the night,
And tuned Lyra's Vega - the summer bleeds

In the sea's cloudstreaks and the wind's new foliage
And all the shapes of sunlight and regret.

OCTOBER: GREEN ECLIPSE

Sitting at the clavichord at midnight,
I hardly make a sound to fill the room,
And could accompany no instrument.
A low light's on; you're sleeping in the dark.

Two wakeful hours ago we watched in awe
The Full Moon in predictable eclipse;
I've never seen such lunar green before,
A starry flue as though we'd drunk much wine.

Why has this color kept me up tonight?
But it's only at night the clavichord's precision
Grows powerful with Dowland's griefs and mine,
And fills the night's lost limits with such green.

NOVEMBER AFTERNOON

I

Although the casement's closed the curtains sway
In the chill wind; the room's gauzy light
Pools and suffuses like old solitude
As if the sky were full of breezy clouds;
You doze, inseparable from the afternoon;
The three cats on the dun coverlet doze.
Now the yellowing iterations of
These illimitable afternoons remain
So placed, like a plucked flower in a vase.

II

Dreams, we know, thus indeterminate,
Cannot be so conjured so to differ from
Waking reality, malevolent,
Bland, pungent, or sedate, but now beyond
A lacune's reordering. One of the cats
Twitches its lovely paws, and breathes out loud.
The afternoon, indoors and aureate,
Is an illimitable dream, in which
The light's as constant as the breezy sky.

III

The casements rattle; the light winds in the wind
To give the curtains the tincture of afternoon;
A cat, eyes closed, pretends to swoon, its paw

Swats a plucked flower in a vase
In dream; asleep you slightly rearrange
The bunched coverlet. Order or disorder:

Let us see, through all the turnings of
The afternoon, how they differ as parts
Of a dull afternoon's ubiety.

IV

The faded pink cosmos in its glass
Has shed its outdoors odor, yet the room
May sometimes seem embued with it as though
It were diffused by low November light
In which the flower sways its feathers. Might
The afternoon be simplified like that?
What more than this slowness ought we want?
The whitewashed walls, the darkened bamboo ceiling -
But the mind is stubborn within its logy buzz.

V

The curtains spread the sun like an autumn cloud.
The finches chirping from somewhere outside
Are those that we expect in April weather.
The cats deign not to hear them. Order or
Disorder? ask the imagos of dream.
Let us for a moment say disorder,
Since every aim is intricately aimless,
And include dull severities of order,

For you and the afternoon to sleep together.

VI

The light spumes like a noiseless cataract
Over the breaks of casement and gauze curtains
To pool in pools of ancient solitude.
The questions of a plangent afternoon
Fade like mist in dull sunlight, or like
The odor of a cosmos in a vase.
The cats lick their paws, their thoughts opaque.
The inspissations of the afternoon
Dissolve to evening chromes, as you awake.

DECEMBER WHITEWASH

December rain drips red dirt
On flaking whitewashed walls.
Soon there's the churned lime smell,
The messy brushes drizzling in the eyes,
The newly wet and dull gray splotches
Slowly turning white in spring sunlight.

SEE OFF MOUNTAIN

The poet and his wife spent the winter of 1984 in a house on See Off Mountain in North Carolina, near Brevard. They had been living in Greece for many years.

REMOTE

My borrowed house is on a wooded hill;
Afar the winter Smokies fade to blue.

A few gray chickadees peck at my seeds
As I go out to split a stack of logs.

The gravel roads are iced; I cannot leave.

Remote to make the restless mind remote,
Even from nature (gray and beautiful),
I watch the valley mist flow west to east
And rise through trees too naked for a name.

Remote - is this the jeopardy I shirk,
A leafwet track too slippery for my tread?

FROST

Each morning speaks its own soliloquy
As light of dawn its daily change of weather.
Lying in bed, we knew there must be ice,
For the squirrels slipped and thumped when on their way
To the feeder. Usually we're up then too
But the morning was too cold without a fire.
Mist through the dark motionless tree branches
Hung so the sky was everywhere, as if
In a glass vivarium. When we got up,
Just chickadees and juncos were at the seeds,
Then tufted titmice and purple finches came.
And ice was everywhere! All through the woods
The weeds and branches and the withered leafstalks
Were sprouting tiny separate cilia,
Minuscule white filaments branched like coral;
Each needle of the huge straight jackpines glittered,
The holly thorns and rhododendron leaves
Were laced with frosted ice as if
The northern note were rendered visible.
Ice so clear the eye caught but a sheen
On wooden deck and gravel walkway made
Excursion treacherous; even the dead leaves
That lay in flattened heaps crunched underfoot
When step by slippery step we ventured out.
Clear casements covered the streampools at the edge
And freezing water flowed over smooth stone
And ice stalactites hung from the mossy ledge
Of rock; even the solitary birdcalls
Rang like chimes as we listened all amazed.
How to make this the landscape of the soul
This common morning in these faded mountains?
Can beauty out of nature be the lost
Proof, sheer ice that cracks a stone? On a post
A bloodred cardinal whistles at the frost,
Then takes a seed and suddenly glides away
Into the mist. This is a day when we

May change things that are deepest in ourselves:
The sun-edged mist will hold the frost all day.

RAYS

Because the light
Rays from the clouds
And melts the white
In winter woods

I close my book,
Lay down my pad
To have a look
And not be sad.

NARCISSUS

Piercing nostalgia from narcissus' scent!
Sipping coffee by the window table
On which a bought narcissus, white and yellow,
Spreads scent like sunlight on the heart's lost shore,
I watch two fluffy squirrels crack our seeds,
And a huge woodpecker pock a frozen tree-trunk,
And morning clouds thin through the bluish valley
Where light from green peaks pleaches in a thicket.
I hold a pencil and a pad of paper
Because my thoughts are sweet and quiet now.
Perhaps there is a boundlessness that vague
Longing alone can reach, suffusing all
The room with distant scent, dissolving like
A soul through nature's unmarked boundaries.

CONNESTEE FALLS: THE IMAGE

We look out over the valley from our mountain
Where Carson's Creek (not named for us) flows toward
Connestee Falls, which winter has made strange
With fine-curved glinting shields of sharp clear ice
Edging water on gray eroded rock:
A tremendous image for the nature we
Trust for its mysteries of mist and thrust
And steady change. No poem or photograph
Could otherwise hold free this single image
From anxious gain and loss, which love holds free,
An image thundering on the heart's gray rock.

MIST ON SEE OFF MOUNTAIN

I peer through thick dawn mist
That ghosts the winter pines
And wait for it to rise,
For the valley to appear
In human clarity;
These are Tohaku's trees
Who meant for me to feel
Communion that he felt
When he gazed on this green
And then took up his brush.

A pair of pileated
Woodpeckers (uncommon
Says Tory Peterson) flies
Through the fine droplet air
From bole to dark gray bole
With shy accustomed ease;
Their pecking punctuates
The mists' breezeless soughing
And parses out the scene
With a sudden sharp rush.

Not every morning gives
Such slow private passage
From close mists' grounded skies
To mountains over there
Across the peopled valley,
Or permits thought that frees
The mind from all self-glooms
That are not tragedy,
Or keeps perception keen
In dawn's remembered hush.

T'AO CH'IEN ON SEE OFF MOUNTAIN

I

T'ao Ch'ien would not have made a garden here
On See Off Mountain looking over mist;
The precinct bounded now by smoky blue
Pine mountains in a curve from north to west
Would show a scholar's garden false, a mere
Displayable virtu:
From what cannot authentically appear,
Even in blur, the scholar should desist,
For winter plucks the boughs to let the dim light through.

Perhaps a clearing for an apple tree
To root, or hacked path through the berry-brambles
Might make good warming labor for a week,
Or anchored stones where nighttime's clear ice crumbles
The once-used way, or just loosens dangerously;
The scholar ought not seek
To trap the squirrel or the chickadee
With his seeds, but to smile even as he grumbles
Ere lapsing into stupid silence, so to speak.

II

Warmed by the fragrant wine, thus mused T'ao Ch'ien:
"I have my house not far from a travelled road
Yet hear no noise of anxious passer-by;
With mind detached, remote amid the wood,
I gather faggots, no thought for my pen;
Up in the cloud-streaked sky
I catch sight of departing flocks again;
If I could find the words to start, I should
Not let these daily truths escape my inner eye."

If the wise scholar could not find the word
What chance have I? No landscape could be more
Instructive even for my feebler thought,
Or have more power to gather and restore
Attention to the mind; tree, hill, stream, bird,

Stone, moss, mist, squirrel, ought
By the enduring nature of such a hoard
Require no further proof that character
Is more than intellect. And then? I wait, distraught.

III

I rise, distraught - although the fragrant air
Is bright, the juncos crackle leaves unseen
Below the porch, and gently undulant
The Smokies opposite bloom pungent green
With pine - and go out to the log-pile where
Are logs to split would daunt
An ax-man who has not so snug a lair
As here; the Chinese music of T'ao Ch'ien
Is in the stroke; inexpert effort makes me grunt.

High in the naked branches sit black crows
(There are not many birds this time of year)
Whose caws are more than sweetly melancholy
But call a grating, deeper note of fear
As if to mock a tree that never grows
In winter gloom, though holly
Nearer the ground glows green and red in snows
And rains and mists. The scholar's mind holds clear
Beneath his usual griefs, his failures, and his folly.

O SAGES

All sages say a mountaintop
Is a fit place to meditate
On loss and on irrational hope
And to know the woods' inhuman bliss
Of ice-edged streams, mulched leaves, and trees
Stark with winter, and they seem right
In their advice. And so today,
The firewood split, the brambles cleared
From long-neglected paths and driveway,
I sit out on the weathered deck
On See Off Mountain so to look
Out on the valley of Brevard
And the Blue Ridge Mountains opposite
As obscuring mist burns off.
But I can't
Repress the sharp, disturbing thought
That passionate involvement is
Akin to airy calm, though this
No reputable sage will grant
In koan or in parable:
That world-attachment may be worth
The risk of inner obstacle,
Of lust and waste and murderousness,
Of those twin serpents wealth and status
That cause the sages' grim rebirth.

All restless now I must get up
Despite the beauty. Two woodpeckers
Glide to a tall pine on the slope
Below, and down on the valley roads
Trucks and tractors move their loads,
And I too have a thousand chores
To do before the evening's study
And joy of books.
O sages, what of
The heart's charged vows to soul and body
Even up in this mountain house?

The turn of a woman's otherness?
O sages, what of romantic love?

SACRED LANDSCAPE

The mountains smoky blue
Repose in green twilight

And the new moon yellow
As a bobcat's prowling eye

And the stars like finches
In the black stripped branches

Here they have caught me
Mid pines and freezing streams

Like any constellation
Here where are no gods

From this eastern forest
A future yet archaic

DRAGON COILS

Dynastic brushes in rich wet monochrome
Induce the mist and clouds on See Off Mountain
To show me sundry shapes on the long Blue Ridge
Then swirl past the lower hills by stream and ledge
And naked rock, that weather's dragon may mount in
Coils to rain upon seeded field and poem:
White flowers on dogwood, pink on cherry sweet
And strong in wind as girls, the coiling skies,
Valley rain in spate, birds' love-sure cries,
Slick mulch-rot of last autumn's leaves, entreat
A man to call his scariest moments home.

ELEGY

Mortality is no lesson
To be learned by heart in a lifetime:
Because of the death of a cat,
I get up, unable to sleep;
The house has gone cold as the night,
The last big log not even glowing.
Outside, the predicted rain
Is falling on woodpile and leaves;
The lights in the valley below
Are out; I leave off my own
Not to shock unaccustomed eyes,
And rock in the dark by the window.
Just a cat. So I grieve for myself,
For the fear that is faithless as weather
And vague as the regular rain.

EARLY SPRING

In the field of white
Sweet wild-garlic flowers
A farmer's peacock struts
And swells his throat by half
And creaks his fierce feathers
Like Joseph's crazy coat
That drove his brothers mad:
A gathered swell of pride
That turned Potiphar's wife
Turns his females' wits.

DAWN MOON

The cold seems universal
In morning moonlight as
The moon glimmers behind
The eastern cloud, until
A fuzzed strip of dawn
Unfurls, scored by the sleeping
Mountain pines, and the moon
Floats in blue not yet
The broken blue of daylight.
Low gray mist abruptly
Vanishes, and a bird
I do not know gives voice
Before the awakening
Of all that is familiar
As ice-film in the sunlight.

WEASEL

The weasel rustles dead leaves
About the ratted shack. He stops, suspicious.
Damp noon sun whets his ice-pick teeth.
He mauls the mountain's plunging shadow
For flesh. Rivulets spread
Beneath the soiled leaves, descend in drips,
A veined delta the weasel knows
In corridors of black and bumps of earth.
Thick rose-trees bend their knots around the stones
As low the weasel bellies by,
Crisscrossing gloom, rapt in roots.

LOOKING FROM SEE OFF MOUNTAIN TOWARDS MT. PISGAH

My Muse may be excused if she is silent henceforth.
--THOREAU

I SEE OFF MOUNTAIN

1

To See Off Mountain robins come
In spring, my first "back home" these graying years
Though new to Carolina's groves; their redbreasts gleam
In the cold and downy godless mountain air, and seem
The moving signs by which the dawn mist clears
And rises through the jackpines' hum.

2

Across the valley of Brevard
Rise mountains where the Blue Ridge Parkway runs
Along the wooded ridge of peaks whose morning hue
Is smokey with a cinquecento-landscape blue;
The raking sun beams through the pines and stuns
Dark leafmold life; the wait was hard.

3

And still is hard. Near See Off's noon
No trace of gods in azure air whose formal
Shapes have formed me out of fourteen years in Greece
By daily friction of the sunlit golden Fleece
Of a Muse; the empty mountain sky is normal
As the redbreasts' steady tune.

4

The telling of each syllable
Of wind or weasel in last autumn's leaves
Or budded maple or dry branches underfoot
Is godless; even water running over root
And rock's no rustic oracle where grieves
The hope of the intelligible.

5

Mt. Pisgah's the most soaring peak
From here - the tourist postcards picture it
Splendid piny blue from a valley pastoral
With cows, horses, and derelict pickup trucks. Hawks call
From Pisgah down to See Off opposite -
Call lost as pre-Helladic Greek.

II Moses on Mt. Pisgah

6

When Moses limped down Pisgah's slant
Forbidden by the weather's God who once
Had welled within him mythically grim as Arab sand
To lean his rockburnt visage toward a grassy land,
Did fixed and bitter words make the magus wince,
Cracked tablets make the tribe recant?

7

The snake he strung up on a pole
To charm the poison of the wilderness
As balm for weary bones - ploy of the desert shaman
Still burning from the desert's bearded bush whose human
Voice still could make him cringe, his face confess
His fright - did not conjure his soul.

8

Say: "I was raised up by God, not cowed."
But what when old and broken for the grave?
A semite wind, a hardening of Pharaoh's heart,
a shining when the shaman set himself apart
Believing he alone was justly brave
Who horns aglow dare breach the cloud?

9

"What Abraham quickened to life
I hardened to the Tables of the Law
On Sinai, since the common tribe could not survive
Nor keep the Ur-born Patriarch's fierce hope alive

On saga, psalm, and rite: Death rubs rule raw
And nature pares with a bloody knife."

10

He shrugged and turned from Jericho
As Pisgah granted him its final grace:
A place of suffering the silence and the error
Of the ark's covenant whose groans are wrought of terror:
His tomb, he whom the Lord knew face to face,
No green-eyed Oedipus may know.

III MYSELF ON SEE OFF MOUNTAIN

11

I wonder where my thought went wrong,
Why, like the eyeless life that damps beneath
A smooth flat stone, I never saw the tumult
That made Aegean shapeliness more than a cult
Of calm, but hung it high a marble wreath
To last a youthful summer long.

12

The robins scatter but a blood-
Red cardinal gleams redder still on the woodpile
Black crest erect before his shyer grayer mate;
Last month I thought, as he preened on the snowy gate
Feigning indifference, to accede to style
Ensanguined by such brilliant red.

13

The world writhes in confusion now,
Or was it always so, and it's just I
Who shirk the hard nobility of tragedy
On See Off Mountain (wrested from the Cherokee)
Or Delion archipelago of sky
And glaucous sea and olive bough?

14

If the gate to the future has
Slammed shut for good (like Dante's door in hell)
Then all our culture is inert, an arcade game
No twelve-year-old would essay twice. The mountain's claim
On the sublime our past disgrace can't quell,
At least no past that ever was.

15

The twisting roads, the switchback creeks,
The leafless dogwoods white with bloom, dawn ice,
Gray squirrels that leap from branch to dripping branch, sharp wind,
Bobbed wrens that run down boles, loud juncos on the ground
Give signals randomly as bone-cut dice:
Gold sense comes from such throats and beaks.

IV Moving Signs

16

Moses on Mt. Pisgah, and I
On See Off Mountain squinting for a Muse
For middle-age, may share a seasoned thought: these fell
Far peaks must loom beyond the long polite farewell -
Though Moses is lawgiver to the Jews
Whose Law I, born a Jew, deny.

17

If lost mountains or middle sea
Yield moving signs that are not stone-scrawled but writhe
On archaic trunks of an abandoned olive grove
Or barnacled shards of a shipwrecked bay, shall love
That's somehow granted shining like a scythe
With age, by muse-means pardon me?

IONIC

κοῦραι Δηλιάδες Ἑκατηβελέταο θεράπναι
Homeric Hymn III

Delian korai, who serve the Far Shooter

spring 1984 - spring 1987

IONIC

Deep down from earth's sweet body
A gush of icy water
Jets us up to thought's
Abstract pediment
And sprays us darkly mazing
To her deep-groved image.

HEROIC SYMMETRY

Swimming past the fine-ribbed sandbar just
A dozen meters from the yellow curve
Of our clean morning beach, whose emblem is
A single palm in a dusty walled-in garden,
Green fronds blade-sharp in the bitter sunlight,
We see the mountains rise like pediments
From which the marble heroes have been hacked
By some daemonic Elgin and then shipped
To the sky for wheeling hawks to gaze upon,
Opaque in dazzle to our human eyes.
But bare forbidding rock that backed their balance
Still lets us sense heroic symmetry
Laid out for eyes that never need to blink.
Though our attention is a paltry thing,
And our emotive hearts throb like a sparrow's,
Such stases are too bitter for grace or glory.
But in the water still and hyalescent
Your full thighs snow as white as lampmined marble
As you tread next to me, a column's sway
In the sweet salt sea's erotic entasis,
The precinct garden swaying in a web
Bitter as dripping lemon or shiny oil,
Bitter as the soul that would be wise
As Herakleitos' damp-defying flame,
Bitter bitter as the fleshless scarecrows
We shouldn't become if seasalt rubbed us young.

The swallows skim for flies above our heads,
A fish shoal flickers by our gleaming knees.
Look! Poppies on the mountains' terraces
Drip bitter blood, and all the ancient tombs
Are shut, and acrid incense of the spring
Evaporates in sun as we swim ashore
With seabrine's bitterness on our red lips.

THE BEACH OF SAINT IRENE

The water of the bay, still gooseflesh cold,
With a fine yellow scum of daisy pollen,
Throws back the sunlight to our averted eyes.
Greek has a word for this: ἀντηλιά
Sunlight opposed, glare, dazzle, sun-brilliance.
The lady next to me, whose nakedness
My squinted eyes slide toward like mercury,
sparkles with light-points even in the shade
From hyaline sandgrains on her back and hips.
The needles of the huge gnarled tamarisk
We're stretched beneath sharpen in the sun.
The daisies burn. The small surf-ripple turns.
She shades her eyes but nothing in her gaze
Is white as the chapel of Saint Irene some sailor
Built to thank the sea for sparing him;
In its flaked whitewash gleam the lost fragments
Of Herakleitos and Archilochos
Which a girl, throwing off her summer peplos,
Bore lightly off in a basket on her head
As she stepped softly on the bird-tracked wavelets.
Tell them to me, tell them to me! Bare, bare
The sea and hills, bare and needing nothing.
I used to say, here was my Ionia;
I say it still, though I am half unsure:
"Stood upon the edge mid wave and wind."
Stunned by the afternoon, we don't put on

Our clothes until the heat-haze subsides and all
The archipelago once more appears,
Melos, Siphnos, Kythnos, Seriphos, Kea,
In seagirt silence in the evening air.

HOMERIC DETRITUS

Last night the bad September sirocco's gusts
Subsided; dawn, I see the surf has spat
Sandpacked stacks of greenish seaweed rotting
On the beach all stiffened and rank. The sea,
Lapsed dull, slides warm and floury thick as soup
Where crabs with surf-gnarled legs twitch hungrily
From their gritty shells. The surface seems rough-flaked
Salt-yellowish. Sea-daffodils are drowned.
A man with a donkey gathers winter wood
Bent waves washed up - it's rotted and no good -
Then scoops up a sack of illegal salt-ruined sand
To roof a coop or stable; his load-backed beast,
Listless here where all is inedible,
Wears a snout-snood to keep the flies that sip
His half-dried gleet from stinging. The gray gulls
Stay on the offshore rocks; fast deadly swallows
Snap up the beach's flies and wasps. Fresh pats
Of ship's oil glisten on the jagged rock
Already darkened with dull blue-green algae.
The wind has piled the seaweed all along
The sand a foothigh ridge, but somehow heaped
Blue plastic garbage-bags all in one place
With dead jellyfish running into nothing.
The sea blind Homer sang in undemotic
Dactyls is cut with the jump of the shallows' pale fry;
He is loth to call the wind-ridged must-dark sea

Anything but treacherous and unplumbed,
And even stilled it hisses like a snake.
I cannot catch the underlying beat:
Is this the source whence singing rhythms come?
Wind-interim's elusive symmetry
Glares blank alike to native and metic.
Brown needles drop from bentback tamarisk trees
Onto the beach's mess. As noon glare nears,
I wish the donkeyman good health and forsake
My swim the last week's wind has kept me from,
Laid low by enervation and by heat.
In the freezing north not weeks away the year's
First dismal rain funnels south though the sky
Is faded blue as an ever empty frieze.

LOOKING FOR TYCHO'S STAR: NOVEMBER 11, 1984

The sky is still our heaven, and we wish
No numbered limits on what we cannot see.
No leaf-streaked colors warm the northern sky
This evening now the weather's snapped to winter
And kept me all day indoors as though at lessons
For the first time in seven sunblazed months.
Just yesterday the sunlight still seemed sure
Though setting south behind Antiparos' peaks.
Such wind! I put on my winter coat
And step outside to look for Tycho's Star;
I'm itchy with an ancient superstition:
Kepler's supernova was our last
Great flash, our galaxy is ripe.
Long black clouds, thrust by the cold northwind
That beats the sea, bends the bamboo, and keeps
Our house-doors closed, occlude the circumpolar
Constellations - it's Cassiopeia I'm looking for,
Where on a cold November 11th in 1572
Tycho Brahe stunned saw a new star
That fabulously increased in magnitude
Till bright and radiant as virgin Venus
And could be seen by day. For four months
He watched it - knew his pretty astrology broken,
Knew church doctrine wobbly now that nothing
Fixed in crystal rings, knew poetry
Of intellect made manly once again

In lyric mode of detailed observation.
The clouds clear for a moment, and the Queen
Who riled Aegean sea-nymphs stretches her white
Gauze-veiled thighs, and withdraws. The winds howl,
The star stays hid, no supernova burst,
For Tyche's formulae cannot be learned:
A knotted thread ties us to limitation.
Before I retreat inside to warm my bones,
From behind the black mountain of Thapsana
The late-phased moon lifts shining where the clouds
Are thin, then vanishes behind the waiting winter,
And the palest moonlight breaks in precious waves
More luminous than the heart could ever need.

FROM THE PAROS DELION

In the cloudless light of noon
Marble melts like snow.
Snails crack black ostraca
That snap like dustripe seedheads.
The twenty miles of sea that lead to Delos
Make burning whitewash of salt
That even the god must shade his eyes
As all the columns fall again.

FORGOTTEN FORMS: TENOS

I

What goddess hides her footfalls under stone?
The dawn is trembling hazed with wariness.
Did some black meteor blast this mountainside?
No castro was ever raised amid these boulders
Where purple thistles spike like sharp-forged iron.
And on the stone hunched crows keep guard as though
Their nunnery concealed some ancient scroll
In magic birdclaw script
Which we would risk all goddess-ire to get
If only we could hear beneath the caws
That mock our Greek stupidity. We turn
From desolation that we cannot scale
And head toward where the Greeks held out against
The Ottoman when the sparse Cyclades
Had lapsed into defeat. These are their bones.

Despite the rubble's garbled lamentation
The past we reconstruct is not consoling.
We scrabble in the stoneheaps of old walls
For bits of bronze, a Latin cross, green shards.
Who lugged these stones to this unfruitful peak?
We feel their fear - it's scary here although
Strong sun and wind have burnt the morning mist.
Venetian Catholics and Orthodox
Were left with rock as their last Occident.

Wind-driven clouds cut short
Our probe for ancient things, and we climb down
With treasure only we would call of worth.

II

White dovecotes resume Byzantine stitchery.
The busy men of Tenos praise their doves
To hint to us the motive freshens deeper,
And we would act the fool to blurt to them
Of Aphrodite's down
Mid these white chapels half as numerous
Where - pigeons perching on the crimson domes -
The goddess grants her glow by other names,
Who in her church weeps tears of human blood.

Our riches are our suffering and pleasure,
But even lovers lack eternity.
The sea is shining in the dolphin straits
From here to Mykonos. An image of
The goddess dreamt and dug up from a field
Of rocks and soil and seeds
Quiets the wind and waves with silver smoothness,
Quiets the mind with rivulets of green,
And all the orgiastic fresh-sloughed snakes
Creep healthy in sodded holes for our good luck.

III

Maiden of Tenos, mother of thy sun,
Who for thy milk's sake does not scorch our hearts,
Let us love long as leaves are green, as stars
Are happy in their ancient firmament,
And wind and waves align themselves in ways
As orderly as human speech may praise;
Let us behold thy beauty which is ours,
Though we are gnarled with death
Like searocks saltpocked on thy northern shore;
Into our common days breathe thy herbed breath
That clears us for the rigors of ourselves;
Let us be pious though thy flesh be hid,
And faithful to the neutral charge of nature;
Though reason crack and intuition quail
Before the lifting of thy thinnest veil,
Accept the wonder of our natural prayer.

IV

Fishing with spear and mask by the ancient mole
Whose sunken marble blocks are smooth as flesh
I start my dives on the wind-protected side
With the ancient masonry still excellent;
But all good quarry is where it's hazardous
So I swim across, green water in my face;
Short waves keep moving me to sharp-edged rock
Whenever I don't think to kick against them,
Although the seafloor garden is astir

With verdant undulations
Like liquefactions of a woman's skirts
As she steps out to gather summer fruit.
I get our dinner, a fine large octopus
Moving from his hole across soft seagrass,
Just when I think I can hold out no more
Against the pressure of the open sea.
As I swim happily to shore, its reddish
Tentacles wrapped tight about my forearm,
I find the first line of a long suppressed
Ionian Anthology: "O goddess,
Whose vines and doves and fruit trees and red domes
Keep Tenos risky in her sweet salt sea..."
I clean my catch, then stretch on the shore to sleep.
Later, as I sit with my wife and friends
In the lemon orchard and we eat and drink,
I tell them what the sea was legending
Who've compassed these forgotten forms before.

NYMPH OF SERIPHOS

He says:

Nymph of Seriphos, eyelid delicate,
This rock is no reflecting shell, nor polished.
Since, lovely as you are, all places reach out to you,
With landscapes fixed for a quattrocento painter,
With seascapes tuned for a Debussy, with all
The arts that men would make your own, why here,
Mid this anfractuous rock, these treeless hillsides,
All scree and dusty thorns where even goats
Are circumspect? Nymph of Seriphos,
Here the sea, even when the northwind
Abates its force, is restless on the edge-up
Boulders, always with an anxious froth
On gray of turning undercurrents; no cool
Cave-ledge here, no smooth suggestive wall to etch
Your symbols; and even stars glint desolate.

Aseid, Napaea, where are no dappled forests,
Hamadryad of the stunted tamarisk,
Dryad where mountain paths are hazardous,
Leimoniad where are no meadows fit for lovers,
Naiad, Potameid, Creneid, Hydriad, these are not pools for girls,
Oread, Maelid, the fruit is thick-skinned,
The boughs gnarled in no informing ideogram,
The cicada's song scratches like nails on mica.

Nymph of Seriphos, why here, where winds
Are harsh and bearded with a rough impatience,
And surf-beat uneven, where wells
Are few and deep and houses huddle on
The high rockspur, whose creatures sing you no measured
Hymn of praise, whose whitewashed walls conceal
Dull red stains of iron and poverty?
Why does your youthfulness choose here, an ancient
Of no sleekness, too hot too cold too bony,
Where the clever youths leave for Athens with no glance
Behind, quick birds for Siphnos Paros Melos?
Where is the bowered garden of your girlhood,
Your marble and your reed-rows and your wreaths?
Yet you are here.

Please, Nymph of Seriphos,
It is for your secret sake I ride the open
Fishing-boat that knows no cause to anchor here,
As dolphins do not stop at sport nor bees
In barren valley, to catch a glimpse of you,
Of foam, of pebbles rounded in the shallows,
Of leaves on sticks that rustle in the seabreeze,
Of nudity that is concealed in brightest sunlight,
That casts no shadow; I limp like Perseus over the stones,
Almost able to recall God's gold
On waiting thighs: Here, nymph of Seriphos,
Here is the precinct you have vouchsafed to appear
To men:

Here I am.

She sings:

The sky and land and sea
Have changed and not changed for
  Eternity
Like any living shore.

The snail-shells' even whorls,
The cowries' sudden gleam,
  Quick eyes of pearls
Along the blinding beam:

It's thus a deep desire
To such as mine is bent,
  And could aspire
To know my full consent.

Noon shade beneath a stone
And pebbles on the sand
  Emit a lone
Ideogram or brand:

It's not by word or glance
That I affect to have,
  But by a chance
That is my self's one wave.

For from the harshness of
Sharp rock that halts the pace
  The rhyme of love
Spreads nets of girlhood's grace,

And in these nets are fish
Or bright migrating birds
  That sing the wish
Of Seriphos for words.

The sky and land and sea
Have changed and not changed for
  Eternity
Like any living shore.

METAMORPHOSIS

Such metamorphosis
Of clamors of the heart
In Sappho's barbitos,
In waves too wild for oars,
In intercolumnation
Of tragic ignorance.

NYMPHAION

The wind that streaked the moon all night with clouds
And changed the way the pebbles streak the beach
Will flow the other way before it's noon,
But in the strange still dawn there's time and space
To build a nymphaion
Of graygreen seawater in the old design
Of columns, mouldings, volutes, and a frieze
Blue behind swirled garments and girls' bodies
Stooping to tie a sandal, stretching to bind a fillet.

It's spring; the water runs too cold for swimming
But the effort of construction keeps me warm;
Bright little fish keep nipping at my legs
And new birds swoop to inspect the lithic forms
For nesting cliffs; the first
Low beat of waves that must precede the wind
Insinuates respect for unfinished things,
And greenhaired Thetis who loves mortal men
Glances with glaucous eyes, and dripping steps within.

NAXOS KOUROS

The kouros in the pomegranate garden
Lies fallen thrice-lifesize with a broken thigh,
Eternally unable to arise,
Unable from his marble pedestal
(Now lost) to chant the Naxians' paid paean
To Delian Apollo, whose thick thighs
Are columned like the temple of his mind;
And we're alone with twenty feet of stone
As birds sing from the pomegranate trees.
Abandoned for his uselessness, he thinks
The rhythmic words; the pomegranates ripen
With clustered kernels like a crimson star
Banded with the galaxy. (As I lay
That time in the roadside ditch, my femur snapped,
The motorcycle revving angrily on me,
My thoughts were clear and effortlessly sequential,
Unearthly tranquil as the god - burst from
Hellenic violence - commands. I could
Not move as I waited for the distant pain
To approach like an army of barbarians.
Lordly, I instructed the farmers who found me,
And lapsed into helplessness.) We marvel at
His huge pocked nudity as a lizard runs
Over the leg's dark crack into the leaves
That have already fallen. The kouros' fists
Stay clenched with concentration that predates

Even his brave Egyptian origin,
Or the clear Aegean blue of his open eyes.

DELOS

As a slow caique took us south past Delos,
The sea transparent and inscrutable
To signify what god is out of sight,
A pair of dolphins suddenly finned out
Between us and the sunken ancient harbor
Whence boats would ferry the dying and the birthing
To Rheneia opposite for a Sister's care;
Their blue backs shedding sudden silver, they
Stayed with us as we angled through the strait:
We had our glimpse - it's all that we may get
And blue enough to say: "Perfection is here
Also; for a moment we were home,
And spoke the fearsome language faultlessly."

THERA: FUTURE FIRE

"Naked we found ourselves on the pumice stone"
Looking south into wind from south of Crete
Welling up strangely hot in gusts and flecks
Of ground that have all future fire to spare.
The island's entrails growl a monotone
Of rust and ashes' sunken memory
As if they yet digested Minos' wrecks.
On the hardening stretch of shore before us black
Small stones grow sun-haze hot and hold in heat
Like coals that char the dry meat from the sea;
The hours hunch in a beach-shrub's wiry shade
From the filed disc. At the beach's thorny back
The mountain with its columns felled like trees
Glints from lightness to midmorning glare.
In spite of dread that peaks at blinding noon
To crater us with the heart's muffled pleas,
A frescoed goddess-wind reverses wind
With ambiguities of rose and jade.
There in the caldera's lava-floored lagoon
Nea Kaimeni rises newly scorched
And glazed, mysterious with jeopardies.

SYROS DAWN

From an old plane tree on the splendid
Seedy main square of Syros town
A thousand sparrows lift at once,
A ripple we can sense, waiting
For the slow dawn ferry to Paros,
Like a sudden salt Aegean breath.

THE GODS WITHDRAW

for Elizabeth on her birthday

I

Though Sun and Moon and Evening Star stay bright,
As we reach for the civilized their gods
Withdraw, and we are left bereft, with ethics
That we must try to order, and cannot,
Like songbirds cut from known migration routes.
Helen's route back was cut. No pinioned swan
Awaited dewy thighs among the reeds.
But Troy was rich in trade, splendid in art,
With salons fit for female wit and beauty,
With gardens where slim reed-rows disperse the wind
For flowering pomegranates and cleft fruit,
For maidens' buds and matrons' blowing roses.
Her raucous kinsmen clattering their armor
Outside the seaward western wall fumed each
Man for himself for honor and renown
(The same to them) or quarreled in their camp,
Petty chieftains ash-daubed with Crete's ruin,
Unable to listen to the earth-rich song.
Tyndareus squandered Helen for a sum
To birds of prey with random bloody talons:
Illiterate braggarts, despoilers and despisers
Of lean serfs whose sweat polished deadly bronze,
Superstitious, thrall to ritual,
With gods who lacked morality and sweetness.

Did Priam, rich in years, let Helen stay
From lust? Or to keep Euxine grain in Trojan
Ships? Or to provoke the barbarians?
From some pattern in Babylon's zodiac?
Or as a gesture of divine aesthetics
("Aphrodite's inimitable gesture")
No pillager thinks deeply serious,
A homage to his city's heritance?
And Priam's rapist son (the Danaans snickered)
Minced eastern and effeminate, no hero,
Yet Menelaos in single combat was
Unable to defeat the dandy. Deadly
He was with bowstring, with lyrestring pierced the heart,
And having judged the naked triad he
Was worthily prepared for her disrobing,
For the fragrances and curtain-muted sunlight.
More than Achilles' prowess Helen claimed,
More than sharpened bronze on the bloody field.

II

The brightest shoot of masculinity,
Apollo, peerless with strung lyre and bow,
And Aphrodite, erotic marine mistress
Of the feminine that lights the world in billows,
Breathed Helen's love alive.
The gods withdraw
And leave in their recession lineaments of
Learned ecstacies of reason and of "love

That shakes the heart the way a whirlwind swoops
On an oak", in rhythms of an intricate song,
In cunning brushstroke and the well-turned shape,
In pleats or tresses fixed to charm a lover,
In ambiguities of numbered thought.
White marble holds the numinous - "But you
Must cut the stone yourself". And lovely Helen
Waits within for our desperate caresses.

III

When Homer, eyes on far Aegean clouds,
Recited nightly to Ionian lords
With plough and scythe and seasurf for his beat,
Did he, beneath ancestral flattery,
Mock them with Paris' excellence and Helen's
Conscious strength of form and brine-sharp mind,
With Hector's tenderness upon the ramparts,
With Priam brave in boy-Achilles' tent,
With fables of the ancient deathless gods
He held in disrespect - so as to seed
A Greek garden to flower with the tended
Grafted to the wild, of watered shade
And sun, of Sappho and Archilochos
Who loved in throbbing metres of the heart?
Lost gods take shape in air as men and women
Dressed and naked. Ethos runs with blood.
Blood of our metres their sole sacrifice.

IV

Helen, Homer chants, chose not to betray
Odysseus in his beggar's rags in Troy:
The man of many wiles with owlgray eyes
Had compassed Troy's high laws and Helen whom
A man needs goddess-wiles to comprehend.
Calypso, Circe, Princess Nausicaa,
Athena, Leucothea, Arete
All melted to his masculinity
And graciousness, that made Greek heroes growl.

The perfect gods withdraw into the aether
But Helen's skyblue veil that fluttered on
Apollo's Trojan ramparts as she walked
(And who could walk with Helen's full-hipped sway?)
Was (let us too make myth) the same that sailed
Odysseus safe ashore on Corcyra
To yellow sand, dried seaweed, and fresh water,
Despite the prehistoric rage of breakers
White with horse-froth, muddy with hecatombs.
Telemachos in Sparta found his manhood
Receiving Helen's veils for his future wife,
And Odysseus from far olive-shaded caves
Returned alone to stony Ithaca
To his heart's own Helen, wise Penelope
(Helen's splendid middle-age exactly,
Forty four), whose beauty and rich portion
Made suitors' blood run red as Agamemnon's.

V

The gods withdraw and leave the poet dumb
Unless he sing within a woman's grace
And "praise her in no cause save verity's",
And so must marry wiser than other men
To find right action in her images:
A radiance that ethical abrasions
Can never dim with suffering or time.
The garden flourishes in summer sunlight,
Vesper shines through the moon's palest veils;
In Helen's kiss the quest for symmetry
Resolves like a flock of doves in morning air,
And makes our moments ring like dowry coins.

THREE FRAGMENTS OF ARCHILOCHOS

I

Holding myrtle sprig and pretty
rosebush flower she rejoiced;
                                        her hair
shadowed her shoulders and her lower back.

II

stood on edge mid wave and wind.

III

Come on with that cup along our swift ship's
benches, unseal the hollow jars and pour
the red wine to the lees; no man of us
can stay sober on a such a watch.

FIGS

Archilochos, sailing from
the Cyclades to Thasos,
made figs, the food of paupers,
stand for the sweetness of home:
"Forget Paros and
those figs and
the life of the sea"
he sang, going by
the rock-cut steps, the angry seabirds,
the precinct hard to get to.

ROSE SCENT

(for Odysseus Elytis)

The scent from roses in two vases
Fills the small neat booklined room
Where I sit prim on a wooden sofa
Ill at ease. The master gives me
Whiskey neat and chats of Paros
Lovely thirty years ago.
Gathering courage I reply
And hear my meagre parts of speech
Abrade in raucous disagreement
Like sharp gulls at a fish, my diction
Shrink like snails in vinegar.
He smiles and says in simple Greek
That one must be a practiced poet
With a heartfelt love for it
To touch the genuine. He signs
The flyleaf of his recent *Sappho*,
Anxious for what I'll make of it,
"With sky and sea, with sun and moon,
With plants and girls, with love."
The scent
Of roses stays with me for days
Across whitecapped Aegean straits
To Paros, home: My last year's work
Must rigorously be redone.
"Love, stories' shaper, seizes my soul

And shakes it like a mountain wind
That rushes raging 'mid the oaks."
The striving after skill, the love
That burns itself in solitude
Fill winter's midnight lamps with oil:
Poets of Lesbos, guide my pen
To ink the inmost cry of things
In song-beat of the genuine,
Release that rose's scent again!

ODE IN DAWN SUNLIGHT

'Ω δῖος αἰθὴρ καὶ ταχύπτεροι πνοαί,
ποταμῶν τε πηγαί ποντίων τε κυμάτων
ἀνήριθμον γέλασμα παμμῆτόρ τε γῆ,
καὶ τὸ πανόπτην κύκλον ἡλίου καλῶ.
--*Prometheus Bound*

I

Slant sunlight, thick with pollen, sparks the horns
On the first bull you see in a field of wheat
At Phaistos in its plain, and lights the grain
Mixed with red poppies, and gilds the storage urns
Of rope-stamped clay, and warms the ivory feet
Of Ida Athena's
Dark slow earth, and combs the foamy mane
Of galloping Poseidon;
Her acolyte, you stride on
Old stones that menace
The owl-glide of your metres' flows and ripples:
Blue ladies, laughing, lift toward you their nipples.

II

Soft Dionysos as the Morning sun
Prods roosters in the ruins of Ephesos
To vaunt at volutes of the sea beneath
The Asian cliff and waken colors on
The waves that compensate you for the loss
Of your Archaic -
Whose sea-coiffed girls with outstretched hand bequeath

Ripeness, whose naked youths
Stride stiff with naked truths,
Whose strict stanzaic
Flow of green replenishes you as if
Lit breakers lasted past the broken cliff.

III

Beneath the high horned mountain and the mounded hill
We plough the field for words again to find
A starting place
And to form the dew and dawn light
White and entire and chill
A second before a god's trace
Widens to azure in the mind
Or gives a slightly stronger tug
On the frayed well-rope
That flips the deep bucket upright,
To feel past nature's hope,
Past the shrewd political shrug,
Past the ancestral book and sacrifice
Into a future's flashed Archaic Paradise?

IV

When Iktinos raised Bassai out of stone
Of no distinction on a distant peak
And formed a column out of glossy thorn
Unthought-of for his city's Parthenon,
It was not to astound you nor to seek

Your rosy east:
When any god in azure air is born
Blackbirds and nightingales
Green the descending vales,
And the white breast
Of sister Artemis is bared in haze
High noon burns off for female solar praise.

V

To praise Hellenic sun aloud? But you
Have never soaked your thought in it the way
A bluegray dolphin circling Delos soaks
His sonar in Apollo's living blue
Descending on his thoughts in a silent ray
Of intellect,
Nor can you plot the April-crossing flocks
Of cranes with shaded eyes
Where distance-piercing cries
The gods perfect
Provide no preparation, plan no sky,
Nor blot the dark tears of the inward eye.

VI

Such deathless facts of recognition may be gods;
But do the ancient ways of wife and wealth
And olive tree,
Of turn and counterturn and stand
Proceeding through our odes

Closewebbed with clouds and earth and sea
And netted thought and noonsun's health
Keep you from being rent like singing
Orpheus still in love
With a lyre's lie, doe's voiced command,
Goddess' homing dove?
What we thought the dawn was bringing
Was something else, unearthly fast,
That now can never die of love, nor loving last.

DELIAN KORAI

[*from Homeric Hymn III*]

A great marvel of undying renown:
Delian Korai, who serve the Far Shooter,
And praise Leto and Artemis of Arrows,
And sing of men and women of past times,
Enchanting all humanity with the hymn,
And imitate the chatter of all speech
Till each of us imagines he is singing.

CAPE SOUNION

I *Poseidon*

You sailors beating north from silent islands
May praise such tensed benevolence when you
Discern my gleaming columns on their base
Of chthonic cliffs, wherein my image watches,
For I transform the chaos of the sea
Whose winds and currents mingle fear and joy.
Here in the bay, my sailors, you may rest
When wind won't let you weather the long cape
And come to pour the honeyed wine from jars
No brine has broached, and pray, and say your words.
The spray-veined columns froth up from the cliff
When you approach, at damp dawn, dazzling noon,
Or sunset darkening to weighty night,
And turn in wind that's flecked with cliffside spices
Where nothing but the waves and you may hear
Our mutual murmurs pulsing in your temples.

II *The Sailors*

Poseidon, great force, shaker of the earth,
And of the seafloor where no crops are reaped,
Lord of these cliffs and of the fierce Aegean,
Tamer of horses with their frothy manes,
Savior of sailors in their pitchy ships,
Uphold the earth, god of sea-swirling hair,
And stretch your sinews in the shoreward wave-run;

Gladden our slitted eyes with Amphitrite
Froth-flanked and curving like the crescent moon.
All beaten seacliffs, all high headlands, all
Long rivers mixing at the molded sea-edge,
All beaches sloping seaward, all rayed depths
Where silver fish flash fins in flowing gardens,
All girls who swim in summer are your pleasure.
O you who love the female earth that bore you,
Succor us who would ply the sea in ships.

III *The Poets*

As we climb toward the colonnade we rise
With slender flutings lacking entasis
And then at last look out to sea and in
To the god's sculpted visage; and we see
Even to the windy Cyclades, our home,
An interval in empty blue of sky
And sea whose surface riffles over wreckage.
Here once the Sounion kouros clenched his fists
Like the daring man who first strode toward the sea
With sea-shapes undulating in his hair
And sea-sounds in the chambers of his ears.
In salty spray, in azure light, in surf,
The marble-gleaming man moves over rockpools
Into the hazard of the light he shares
With formed divinities, a light that is
The only human immortality.

JUNE NIGHT

The salt wind falls past midnight,
Rises, dies, and you
Can hear the channel's currents maze direction.

Black surface. Nightbirds. Metallic stars
Separate in the made-up constellations.

And when you turn

The sea itself steps on damp sand,
Shakes like a beast
Whistles like a bird,
Waits for another sea to answer.
Indolent.

Nymph, nymph, you say,
Genius of one night only.

HER HERAION

I

Blazed structure of this archipelago
Is your noon Heraion, and you are here
Because its formed perfection proves your own,
Because its skies are blue, its waters clear
As thought that moves in flowing gists as though
Such movements could explain the tragedy
Or lyric cry, its rigorous patterns hone
A single day to some completion that
Stays static and alive; for you such free
And human longing must seem frail and flat,
Whose every moment is a polished stone
In sand, in surf, in green depths of the sea.

II

This rooted rock is a moveless stereobate
For columns of your body's exact noon
Wherein all youth and age are quick compressed
By hymning light; your heaven, hell, full moon
To a static phase enclosing tragic fate
As a female coolness silvering the heat;
For light wind eddies on your hips and breast,
And slightly lifts your lustrous hair, and lays
Hazed gold on all the valley's stubble-wheat,
And ripples on the island straits and bays,
Till all the archipelago is expressed

By shell-shapes of your sea's unrestless beat.

III

Though Naxos, Andros, Melos, Sikinos
Compose a frieze for you that is a dirge
For origins whose ends are adamant
And bitter-rank to taste as mountain spurge,
Though Siphnos, Tenos, Kea, Seriphos
Raise a pediment that deceives all rhyme
To thinking grief for manly voice to chant
With deep restraint, you are a beckoning woman
Whose honey lures loud bees like flowering thyme,
Who in your open Heraion gleam human
With fine erotic flesh and thought, to grant
To earth, wind, sky, and sea a sunlit prime.

IONICON

Although we smashed their statues,
although we drove them from their temples,
not for this at all did the gods die.
O earth of Ionia, they love you still;
their souls remember you still.
As an August morning breaks upon you,
vigor of their life passes through your atmosphere;
and sometimes an aetherial youthful form,
invisible, crossing quick,
passes over your hills.

--CAVAFY

COVE

I

"Time is a moving likeness of eternity",
A fanned light upon the sea at noon
From the round metaphysical sun, by analogy,
That flashes the collapse of time into its opposite
In a certain moment, a continuous instant,
Protecting us from what might have been
What might be yet in brilliant blue
What cannot be forgot, in bitter blue.
Astronomers and divers offer praise
And yet we are afraid. Accept
Our praise. By the stupendous cliffs
Our little boat (the *Sappho*) prows the wavelets
Pellucid when the wind falls back and we
Descry the blue of sky flame into beams
And break upon seasand, searocks, and seaweed
Undulant a dozen meters down
So radiant that in Platonic blue
Disruption of the outboard stops
Going past a chapel's promontory
Where a seacliff coast recedes to clarity
Along rock-lines haze-droplets have made glisten
Cormorants veer by in silent scudding
Gleaming gulls fold motionless on spurs of rock
And distant loomings of the archipelago
Correct their shading like new memory

In Aegean azure, haze of heat.
A pair of eagles soars from olent cliffs
Offers its deception:
Over there our gods are over there
Invisible but felt like danger forming,
Follow silent so they take the likeness of such blue
And toss anchor, take a swim
In this cove of sunlight
With its wake of mermaids, silver dolphin wave,
Shells of a woman's body, green tended garden
And as you mingle illusion and recognition
Embue your flesh with its salt of fact,
Hypostasis of water and of sunlight
That filled with blue and green and speckled
Your shadow underneath the rocks,
And when you face away from this deception
The eagles wheeling past a blocked horizon
It will not ever again be so easy
When all the moving likeness and the blue
Shimmer in your memory at once.

II

Is the island labyrinth the way to find
The symbol for a goal that cannot be said or thought?
Because there is no way to know when we are truthful
We make a method that is not a method
And call it "lyrical action" out of the need
To utter something not in our own voice.

"You mean the word of knowledge which has a living soul
And of which the written word is no more than an image?"
Yes.
    No.
        We seek
Rhythmic signs that render Time
Sensible to human understanding,
That turn an idea's flutter
Into a bird that we can really see
Flying to sing from a wind-gnarled snakewood tree
Or fish into a nymph whose female flesh
Explicates the sunbeamed mesh of noon;
And in such hopeless metaphors, such transformations,
Where one term is always like a rock submerged,
The sun's first day is lovely in our measures
According to the measure of the heart.
When we would say, capsized by a symbol, "cove",
It is because we would say "love".

III

Is it a poet's praise you want, and rhyme?
  Nymph, I would blow my triton's horn
  If what I know when I'm seaborne
    I could know all the time.

Slow sages chant that oceans have no end
  Yet floors and reefs and rocks appear
  In bays and shallows green and clear

For poets to commend.

Although these distances belong to you
Beyond what I conceive, such room
Is overvast to be my tomb
With its unmuted blue.

And when the *Sappho* glides us to our bay
For sun-edged dazzle at the stroke
Of noon, her body is the book
Whose verses flow away.

IV

All living things are sessile
To the invisible.
We paint the *Sappho* white because
We cannot walk or swim, cannot
At morning, noon, or afternoon,
Sun low on cliffs or burning in the sea
Or glowing low among the Cyclades,
Reach a known starting point,
Around the promontory with its chapel
To the saint whose icon is the sea,
Without her, by analogy,
By logic, by equivalence
(One term submerged, the shell
Toward whose hidden gleam we dive),
Unless by natural grace; the cove

Is closed by love as by an eagle's ceinture.
A light upon the blazing sea at noon,
In pools glaucescent as her eyes when she
Looks at me and past me into air,
Is no rare thing, but common:
So drenched by infinity, never have I,
No never, been so attached to life.

IONIC FISH

Fear of death and tragedy
Make even the doomed sun shine.

The sea and sky, the rock and stone
Of luminous perplexity,

Coins of olive leaves and rain:
Emblems of awe. In the sea

Ionic fish leap again,
Their scales silver and shimmery,

Ornamental flashes. Be
Afraid aright, reflecting man.

FROGS AND SWALLOWS

1986-1993

COINS

On the sea the rain
Mints its countless coins
Stamped with images
Of simple sanctity -

A pomegranate and
The palmtree of the year.

SADDLE SHOES

I used to tiptoe on my father's polished
Saddle-shoes to see out the back window
Of the yellow trolley screeching us to
The Bronx Zoo. I don't remember the zoo.
On the return trip he would buy a cigar,
A Sunday paper, and a treat for me
At a chocolate-colored candy store. He was
Much younger than I am now and handsome.
I have not seen him now, a small old man
A long plane ride away, in years. We write.
A poet's life brings no consoling money
In its gnawing laziness to pay for all
Nostalgia's sudden sadness and clarity,
Or to buy saddle-shoes as fine as his were.

UNLACONIC GREEN

Fortune's kiss
that lasts a century
(Mozart Keats Massaccio)

Leaves little marks
on your
yet unravaged cheek

Snow on Taygetos
from the unmarked
Laconian plains
miles of oranges
watered earth

It is hard to decide
what to think about
when you look away

The rain on the mountains
moves
through the ravines
dragon-dark

Hesiod praises God for it

The wildflowers bend but
cannot be hurt

Little mark on anemone petals
enduringly beautiful
like clouds or asphodels
in their green rayed fields

shells on the peaks

that Leonardo thought about

Things change

Jeopardy and risk risk and jeopardy

(Shun not the honed cliches of epic poetry)

Black Fate

The gods are not to blame there are no gods

Take your chances

Hesiod warns take your chances

Myrtle celandine field-marigolds

(Shelly Bazille Pergolesi)

It is hard to decide what to think

about that snow on Taygetos

has no intelligible footprints

nor Leda's nor God's

The rain moves down

These dark ravines

And mists the town

With winter's greens

Very orderly

Little yellow celandines

along the stream

Myrtle on the neat rock wall

Sparta was stronger without walls
but not strong enough for lyric
We still are horrified
Plato loved her
(whose politics were about
as trustworthy as Pound's)
Taygetos' shadow touches Eurotas
and the reeds
Unmarked fields of rainwashed oranges
Gypsies in the Agora that never was much to speak of
And Tyrtaios from blue Ionia
"shake your fearsome crests at them"
Taygetos huge with snow

Fortune's bland kiss
though inevitable
(Georgione Crane Schubert)
Is not divine
trust the ancient poets
chanting from memory
of inevitable
risk and jeopardy
Black Fate
Nor love nor hate nor any human thing
Nor Symplegades nor the shifting pebbles

The old goddess
Eurythmia
sees with shining eyes
with tragic eyes unblurred

Helots furrow the ground
blandness furrows the brow
Not even thought (as we look away) can open

children's graves

And the clear air of birds reflects

in endless arcs

undifferentiated Fate

Magpie cuckoo nightingale

Swoop in repetition

"Orchids

Snow on Taygetos

melting on the donkey trails"

A few words in a note book

And again "love

strife"

Our glance from here to there gleaming

"There is no mortal who can

escape evil of nature

or evil of himself

or risk and jeopardy"

The olive trees give shade to gypsy tents

And goats also enjoy the ancient masonry

weathered dull

And the moving coils of rain and hidden logos

Titian

Verdi

Aeschylos

"I can neither be silent nor can I speak"

Snow on Taygetos

Unlaconic
Clover sparkling in the mist
Annihilating all to
Green

ROWING

As we row across the harbor
Quiet as we're able
From dark deeps the sunlight
Rises like a loosened seaplant
In the changing current.

FIRST RAINS

I

The first day after autumn's longed-for rains
New mushrooms in the turned unplanted fields
Spread big and ridged enough to pick; the sun's
Slant rise along the dimming arch regilds
The dying vineleaves; the speckled lizard runs
Slowed on his rubble wall; a farmer wields
His hoe on darkened clods, spits on his hands,
And grunts in metres bedrock understands.

II

Green weeds! Yet we have months of wind and cold,
And sea-air pitting leaky window-frames,
And glooms no powers close to man withhold,
And ranting in the starless night, bent beams,
Dim neighbors' lamps, June's whitewash streaked with mold;
When riverbeds declare forgotten aims
I, indoors again, labor to control
Torrential metres of the flooded soul.

III

Am I a Platonist like Einstein who
Presumed there's "something that our mind can't grasp"
Except in keen reflections gleaming through
Created images? Or better clasp
The hand of ignorant Montaigne who knew

Too much, whose Que scais-je polished the rasp
Of years? The formal garden of Epicurus
Trains shrubs up crumbling walls that half immure us.

IV

Shall this generation waste all on arms
Like Pharaoh stuffing billions in his tomb
To overwhelm the decadence of forms
With talismanic permanence? I am,
Though generations have trod through all alarms
Of bloody Alexanders at their game
Of murder, all aghast at an ultimate greed:
Those dying generations writhe and bleed.

V

In Shakespeare, Dante, Homer, we are less
Regarded than a pauper's ghost; that's why
We breathe anew within them and confess
Our character; when Piero and Hsia Kuei
Brush on a landscape glazing human fervor -
All wrought of contrapuntal sea and sky -
Is it because our common pains conceal
The coiling tragedy that lights the real?

VI

Last fall the first downpour was plentiful,
But winter brought northwinds withholding rain,
And by July our wells were muddy; shrill

Cicadas scratched our trees; our yield of grain
Was meagre. Now few purple olives fall
On ground that's soft enough to dig again:
I take my hoe, spit on my reddened palm,
And dig the garden in the darkening calm.

ATARGATIS OF ASCALON

Her silver fishtail undulates
In her tended pond
While in her shaded temple precinct
Consecrated whores and eunuchs
Collect the silver coins
Imprinted with her images and signs.

Admire her girlish breasts
Gleaming through the pool's jeweled ripples,
But touch a dove, the beating flesh
And feathers, and die. You know
The ancient rules: Admire, pay, abstain.

MONK AND POET

"God's daughters breathed in me a voice
Divine, that I might celebrate
What is to come and what is past."
Bringing back his Hesiod
And St. John Chrysostom, both
In mystic Greek, I knock and call
At the old Taxiarch Monastery
Where Brother Jacob works alone.
Up against an unfarmed hill
Its rough stone walls are damp and draughty.
He nibbles Lent's salted olives
And twice-baked bread and offers me
Dried figs and wine, while I tell him
The state of the world according to
Radio reports and magazines;
We nod sadly in ignorance.
He seeks repentance and communion
With God, I the goddess behind Him
Whom Poetry claims to disturb.
He's closer. When we say goodbye,
We're standing in a field of purple-
Blue lupines and white asphodels.
Across the distant bay is hazy
Naxos, I go the other way.
"The right time in all things is best",

But every thought dissolves in time,
Only longing keeps up with the flow.

"GO PLANT THE DAISIES. . ."

I

"Go plant the daisies of your tomb whence ye were born";
  What's to recall now drowsy summer's here?
Bugs lie in golden grass, and swallows skim the corn.
  Sunlight is democratic: You must fear
Not its intentions toward snail-slime or shrivelled horn,
  Toward flesh and warping bones and bleaching hair,
    But blindness. Brightness that's too dense
    Dims praise of sense and lack of sense.

II

Shrubs of wild daisies wither by the dusty road,
  But in the garden, glowing yellow-white,
They drink wellbucket water of the springtime flood
  After the dust has vanished with the light,
And convert the drilling sunbeams into green shade
  Where sleeps a cat whose rat-friends stir at night.
    By moon or sudden stars you can
    See daisies where your day began.

III

Mid a citrus orchard's greens darkening to duns
  A blackbird and a golden oriole
Sing to gnats and moths in the light of setting suns
  Of sunken things whose surface is your soul.
Three goats wake up, a donkey brays, a dumb calf runs

As though his hobbles stretched, trips in a hole,
Gets up and runs. A thousand grains,
Issued from dust, scatter like rains.

IV

But equinoctial light that gulps the greens and gleans
The slightest glint of independent hue
With gleaming scythe and floods the season's quoted scenes
With glare, leaves the grainfield where, shambling, you
Praised daisies in their youth, and where a figure leans
Bent low against the gnarling wind, close to
The crackling dried-up daisy heads,
Seed-burrs, and rings of poppy-seeds.

V

Two crows atop a twisted cypress tree don't seem
To mind the brightness that obliterates
Proportion, color, and defining shadows from
Your hill and house and beach. They caw their hates
And furl black wings tipped with wet ash: No midnight dream
Is blanker that on waking dumbly states
With a more cautious, raucous voice
The dire inequities of choice.

VI

The salty air is colorless. Your absence is
Apparent even to cicadas' clicks
That, burning nuclear fuel of the sun, won't cease

Until the core explodes and flares and wrecks
Itself with time. What if the epigraphs of Greece
Exalt entanglements of death and sex
In metres easy to forget
Till even your day's-eye has set?

VII

Globe thistles and Corinthian acanthus keep
Their colors all along the mountain walls
Where even goats leave them alone. The sea's asleep
With one eye open like an animal's
And breathes in rhythms swirled up from the fishy deep
So you can only tell by beach wavefalls
How fast a foamy god can fake
Another name and stay opaque.

VIII

"And name the sun an emblem for the whirling wheel
Of change, to blazon Mutabilitie",
And blow the dewy daisy open to reveal
God's polished threshing-floor ringed by a sea
Whose salt pickles the primal ruins. Then will you feel
Your blood race with a cosmic piety
By crouching in a wormy tomb
And calling it a virgin womb?

IX

Blind as a baby stuffed with milky Hera's breast -
  Because a goddess-glow fires air too bright
For rational advances, and the hero's quest
  Seeks something else, seeks monsters of the night,
Of chaos past earth's rim, of islands of the cursed,
  Of earth's black guts, but never here, in sight
    Of common love - you bawl a wish
    You could be deathless as a fish.

X

A daisy-wreath that's hung up on the door is round
  As any sea. "Go plant the daisies of
Your tomb whence ye were born". The richer ground,
  Half-shaded by a grapevine trained above
To winnow sunrays even of cicada-sound,
  Needs your thoughtful compost. How else is love
    To flourish till the day you die
    With tragedy's sharp dry-eyed cry?

XI

At pointed dawn or dusk you tend your daisy patch
  While Scops owls with electric note repeat
Whole epics of what can't be said. The moon keeps watch
  And drives you just as mad as light and heat,
And sets a sapphire-misted crescent on a swatch
  Of sand, a ghost of mystery. But what
    You hush before old mysteries

Gives stiff emotions and stiff knees.

XII

Midnight and high noon are terrible for the still-
ness of the soul. Blankness blazons its mark.
Shape it like a common daisy and its sunsmell
At noon or ghost-scent in the furling dark
Swirls yellow pollen in the air, the hair, the well
Whose changing level comforts with a jerk
Of welcome and reflects your gaze
With cool wet ripples on your face.

TRAGIC

I *Pieter de Hoogh*

De Hoogh loved clarity of air and light
In good Dutch rooms under a woman's reign;
He kept himself outside them that he might
Put only logic there; he died insane.

II *Robert Lowell*

Proud of your family, and hating it,
You were condemned to write about yourself.
From this no fierceness, craft, or dedication,
No ecstacy religious or insane
Could save you. Not sorrow. Not humility.

III *Monteverdi*

We dropped a red rose on your grave
As do all who crave tragedy,
Its raving tune of sanity.
A rose was there, the blood is fresh.

TO DELPHIC APOLLO

I

Bereft of even silver-age romance,
We still strain to hear oracles from you.
It seems we think them up and tell them to
Ourselves, to feed the mind with more than chance
Or choice in this or that, as if the blue
Above the sea of olive trees
And glitter of the strait would please
You through the numbers of a serpent's dance.

II

You fought to interpose your forthright gaze
Between the deviousness of the descant
Earth's Lady in her graciousness might chant
To lulled malingerers in her metric maze,
And us, reworking it to what we want
To hear when we're awake: the lyre
Of truth beyond the heart's desire
That twists us through black nights and blazing days.

III

We bring no laurel for your pythoness,
No myrtle; such rules never stay the same;
But still your sunshot arrows prick us lame
In our approach. Unready, minds a mess,
Too choked with chatter for any sacred name,

Unjustified in all belief,
Unsanctified by joy or grief,
We still may feel the clefted presence press.

IV

Snow-pure Parnassus overhead, whose face
Affects the west, flows like a suckled breast
With streams in rocky caves. What presence pressed
When you, distrustful of her skirting grace,
The sweet and threat of her caresses, cast
As if rationally inclined
To contrive a temple to your mind
Above the cleft that wafts throughout the place?

V

Resplendent light when Leto's lovely twins
Force the futility of their attacks
On seasons' rot and root, on greenish cracks
In marble symbols. And the planet spins
From any point but here. Hawks call to hawks
As they decline from hidden nests
On cold Parnassus' haunted crests
That there is no forgiveness for past sins.

VI

Priests told the Apostate's king, whose purity
Offended all, that here's no secret cell,
No verse-muttering spring, no cadenced well,

No girl to chew the bay of prophecy;
He wept. But who's in tendence now to tell
That truth to us, as it infers
Neat dactylic hexameters
From stream and stone and bird and shading tree?

VII

Will wept-for gods return? See, they return,
And drink the blood of earth's prophetic breath
And terrorize us with repeated death.
You thought by being distinct, harsh, and stern
To let us die in ignorance. Your wrath
Proved weak. This high and holy place
Is breathing with a previous grace
That you can't hide, that somehow we must learn.

VIII

Who sings at dawn wrapped in the dragon's coil,
You know. And on the paving-stones faint hoof
Beats animate archaic ways of truth,
As written. Olives gleaming with their oil
(As gleaming she is aging into youth)
Make sunlight black as they reshine
It into flesh. Take word and sign
As they do from the earth's dark-sharded soil.

APHRODITE ON MELOS

Because I am timid do you think
I would not steal a glimpse
Of your body in or out of robes?
That glare protects your lambency from metre?
That shade is a green veil for your goldglare?

These bees will not sting drunk on poetry,
Sunlight, and shade, in crooked flight and buzz;
And premonitions of the hot cicadas
Do not deafen the least tendrils of song;
The wasps are laying eggs in purple figs.

From your terraced hillsides
And your apple trees
The whole bay of Melos
Shapes your melody.

NAMELESS

We trust the name Apollo when it is
The hope of light and art and intellect,
And trust his lustfulness and circumspect
Disdain for nymphs and nameless goddesses
Of dubious demesne. Our sun is his
Whenever thought is clear; he has not wrecked
Our sureties nor led us to reject
Our doubts: skies azure over the abyss.

So, nameless smiling Lady, mistress of
Black Soil, green earth, white sheets, who would deny
The tenderness and terror of your love,
Whose metrics sharpen as they live and die?
Let us sometimes depend on him, to move,
Within your means, to his more simple sky.

RELIGIOUS DRESS

Shorts are made
For boyish play
And blockade
The sacred way.

Mini-skirts
Rise in a breeze
That asserts
The Mysteries.

BENCH PRESS

I lie unwilling on the cheap weight bench,
My muscles in a preparatory clench,
And look up (warm-ups do not help) to see
200 lbs. of metal mocking me.
Why do I do it? To pump up my pecs?
To broadcast odors to the weaker sex?
To let off steam? To hold old age at bay?
To keep the devil Listlessness away?
Because my life is dull, my mind a mess?
No. I grip the bar, breathe hard, grunt, and press.

THE WRONG GOODBYE

Among the filthy boats
Listing with scrambling mobs
One more hot summer ends.
In my old swimming trunks
I see off summer friends
Heading to humdrum jobs.
The dock policeman notes
Cute girls in acute funks.

Fresh money's greased the place
With rash excess of sun;
New dollars ooze cement
That flakes in early rain,
And enemies relent
Not out of hate or fun
Or old-time's saving face
But to repair the drain.

Even the beachbare girls
Reeking of cocoa oil
And not of sea or weed
Cannot collect the light
December's toilings need.
The ship's frayed ropes recoil
As the propeller whirls
Dredged water milky white.

"Cheap rooms" hawkers declaim
To Germans disembarked
Too late to make the scene.
I dodge the chaos of
The dock and sneak between
Stalled fish- and fruit-trucks marked
By a bored driver's name.
Inertia makes its move.

What if, in winter gray,
The wrong goodbye takes hold
So "home" miscalculates?
If closed shops and hotels
Stay dumb and deaf to Fates
And do not shrink with cold?
As two boats chug away
The old church rings its bells.

FOOTPRINTS

I

What holds me to this sea and rock,
This vineyard, field, and olive grove,
That with an inward shrug I love
Them more than maplewoods and brook?
Is it in freedom or in thralldom that
I name Athena when her maids forget?

II

Zeus in the lovely legends sired
On ladies, nymphs, and girls a slew
Of children that he never knew
Grew to desire all he desired,
And dying in the blood of ignorance
Doubted his wisdom, damned his dominance.

III

When I was green, those grand old men
Would prattle of experience
And wisdom to my prurience
They feared would try to change again
The vicious state of things; it made me mad
They hated changes whether good or bad.

IV

Lewd Dionysos, prim Apollo,
Dark Christ also, fled from Amor
Who sang what psychic flesh was for
But not the agony to follow:
Poets, Scholars, Beauties with hair unfurled
May not neglect to praise the dying world.

V

The mind's lucid perplexity
Undaunted by the moonless night
Glimmers with a living delight
Like phosphorescence in the sea;
I do not seek myself among the stars
By which the dreaming fish arrange their wars.

VI

Temples sunk into granite graves
Are plundered grave-goods for the land;
The island's Elements command
The dripping goddess of the waves
To stand on cliff or plain and slowly turn
To set true measurements a man may learn.

VII

Since pessimism and despair
Are not akin I turn my back
Upon decrepitude's attack,
The universe in ruins; there
Are pending matters to be put aright
That burn the midnight oil another night.

VIII

A pillar where a shield's agleam,
A snake in crumbling wall, a bird
With gray eyes: thus the mind is stirred
To counterpoint the pre-formed theme
With something not itself; so that Amor
Must pipe a figure he has heard before.

IX

So when the song bleeds from too deep
In me, I change its mode and measure
And plan it for a woman's pleasure;
I shun the error that would weep
Soul-shrinking tears and strut the words as magic
That's adequate to joyful awe or tragic.

X

Athena, with an open rose
That smells like sea and mountain air
Infused into an essence rare,
Leaves soft small footprints where she knows
Even a man who ducks his simple day
May ponder on them should he pass that way.

THE CHERRY TREES AT HAGIOS IOANNES KAPAROS

Dante imagined earthly paradise
A maiden picking flowers by
A brookside; doubting Homer, wise
With tales, filled it with asphodels; the sweet
Angels of Angelico greet
New souls with trumpet, drum, and psaltery.

But I know it's a mountain garden where,
In walled and watered fields below
An old white monastery, pear
And apple bloom in april sun, where quince
And walnut flowerets sweeten sense,
And tendrils of wind creep through a cypress row.

But most the terraces of cherry-trees
All hung with maiden-white allow
To angel presences and bees
Staggering through bee-din with yellow loaves
And us the blossom-waft of love's
Lasting moment that's made visible now.

What if this distant garden is a mere
Image or hopeful reverie
That I have half-imagined for
A dimmer time? The wise masters are right.
Circled in shade, we snatch delight

In a green kiss beneath a cherry-tree.

So paradise is a cherry-grove in bloom.
The gardener, who's not as old
As his hands look, who we assume
Has labored here by choice, brings us a glass
Of wine. "In eighty days", he says,
"There will be cherries; picked at dawn, they're cold."

BEES

The bees go crazy
In spring.
Every dripping flower
Is too much for them.

Too much, lazy
As you are, for you.

Flowers droop with bees
And with the sound of bees.

BUNTING

The bunting on the wire
Announces his desire
So repetitiously
You'd think he was not free
To stop and fly away.
Instead he sings all day,
A poet and a lover,
To flush the hens from cover.

DAISIES

The daisies are so warm in air
It smells of daisies everywhere!

SHE WADES

She wades
The salty shallows of the cove
So clear in sunlight that the sudden shades
In floating patches like a temple garden's
Of rock and seagrass prove
The crazy insubstantiality
Of burdens
The mind casts carelessly into the sea.

Small fish
Lured by the whiteness of her thighs
Too sharply kiss the coolness of her flesh,
The tiny shrimps her toes, so that she can't
Stay motionless; her eyes
Connect her to a tun shell's nacre-glow
Aslant
Upon a mica rock three feet below.

She bends
And lifts the lovely whorlèd shell,
Which since it is so perfect she intends
To take back to the beach and home, into
The blazing air. All's well,
Until she feels it move: a hideous
And new
Creature emerges hapless in distress,

And switches
Its slimy orange tentacles,
Drips acid from its horrible snout, twitches
In dry light as it starts to suffocate.
Three distant terns or gulls
Scream and spiral down as with her white arm
Stretched out
She puts it back, careful to do no harm.

For each
Burden pitched by the restless mind
Into the still cove from its curve of beach
Something is hooked unknown before. Now she
Steps naked with her kind
And graceful movements grasping something from
The sea
And shows a ravaged coin of Byzantium.

DESPOTIKON

Despite chipped blades of black obsidian
  And unglazed shards of pottery,
Despite a rifled tomb of rough-hewn stone
  And inlets wind-chipped from the sea,

No one has ever holed up here for long,
  Not even for some half-starved goat
Beard wagging for a tinge of green among
  Dry rock and thorns. And yet our boat

Moors here, and spooks the pygmy cormorants
  Out to sea with the gulls and crows,
Since heading home we glimpsed, wind-gaze askance,
  A whole hill filled with white rockrose.

DECEMBER

December. In a month
A strange new year. In two
The blossoming almond trees. In three
Sunlight on Aegean waves
Yellow with daisy pollen.

And as always
The tragic marble gleaming through the summer.

VILLA ROSPIGLIOSI

I

The frog pond at the Villa Rospigliosi's
Almost dry this warm September; there's been
No rain for months; all Tuscany is dry.
A few frogs leap among the waterlilies'
Tattered leaves whose shade seems hardly green
Or cool or thick or deep enough to make
Them safer from the mottled yellow snake
Who hunts them with extinction in his eye.

II

In fertile times the mountain's water must
Have flowed from spring to lion's mouth to pond
To basins in the rose-twined entrance way,
Gladdening ear and keeping summer's dust
Damped down, before it gurgled into the ground
In runnels for vines, trees, and vegetables,
And flowers for the panelled entrance hall's
Polished tables. Its echo cools our day.

III

The ruling monastery up the hill,
Whose much pruned olive-trees arch Romanesque
On old properties bounded by stones and rows
Of male and female cypresses, keeps all
The meager trickle for its garden. A brisk

Breeze from the blue-tipped Apennines blows sere
With no scent of the fortune of the year
Whose color every trellised vinestalk shows.

IV

On the raised parterre behind the formal garden
Two nymphs of age-streaked marble proffer grapes
And classic breasts that careless draperies bare,
Above the grotto-lion's stifled guerdon
Of running water. The fountain's graceful lips
Unmossed attract few doves; its stillness proves
The painter's convocations of blue Loves
Want all our pagan hearts to flutter there.

V

The garden's two magnolias, higher than
The house, have thick gnarled trunks, green shiny leaves,
And prickly cones for fruit. House swallows chase
About them frantically at dusk and dawn
Though they would rather sleep beneath the eaves
After their evening's twittering insect flights;
While twilight's on the mountain niche the night's
Begun for them. Tiny bats take their place.

VI

Reapplied since the sixteenth century,
The villa's ocher wash is stained with drought.
(In those days all the lordly families

Took orders from the Spanish Medici.)
The villa's ordered fields are rented out
And so the watered peach and pear trees bear
Exportable fruit; for pleasure's sake we share
Red roses' fragrance, falling to our knees.

VII

At dawn the owls and guinea hens give cry
Before we're half awake; the sated frogs
Lie low; the bats return; the silent swallows
Suddenly leave; the lightening of the sky
Spreads on Prato; the farmers' lazy dogs
Patrol their plots; sun jogs old bells and fills
Old churches hidden in the wooded hills
And songbirds start up in a thin stream's willows.

VIII

With the green shutters open from our room
Pistoia's mapped-out plain, the light's prospect,
Saint Zeno's dainty campanile and
The Humble Madonna's Brunelleschean dome
Settle upon the sensual intellect
A symmetry whose measurement of blood
Slightly distorts. And where the mind has led
Nature rededicates the lay of land.

IX

The blue, the rose, the white, the tan, the gold
Of a saint's trecento altarpiece are in
The land and mountains, passing clouds and air,
So that its life glows unretouched and old
With a harsh grace. Again the bells begin
To toll for us, that happy we do not
Demand more of ourselves, compete with what
We've brought with us, delight in what we dare.

X

Days of thick clouds, then rain. Good rain deceives
The trees and grass with its lit intensity
Of air. Next dawn the lion's roar persuades
The frogs to boom their praise from lotus leaves,
Ignoring snake and us. Night owls are free
To hoot by day. Edible mushrooms sprout
And lawn flowers too. At noon, while we're still out,
A gladdened sun rounds us in lights and shades.

IONIAN IRONIES

I

Green waters of the bay, blond beaches' wrack,
Aegean wind that blows from where you bend
Until another island blows it back,
The cypress tree that burgeons all its cones,
Complexity too great to comprehend
Unless in parables of rocks and stones
Are, when their earth-tapped source trickles to mute,
Re-ramified by Homer's word and root.

II

Was Homer blind, who mocked the gods, who showed
The Trojans thrice more civilized than Greeks
Encamped for spoils upon the fertile Troad?
Does Chios or little Ios hold his bones?
Has there ever been a bleached bone that speaks
Lost epics, elegies, or even groans?
The stories Homer told still seek their date
In Greek that's literary and ornate.

III

Archilochos and Sappho worshipped sex
In thrilling rhythms so rose-scented that
They had to form their verse to unperplex
The fickle goddess and the god of fact
Dazed on a throne or golden chariot,

And the heart whose daemons make the good abstract;
They were condemned for giving tongue to waves
Beating a beach grown with abandoned graves.

IV

Thales decocted water prime enough
In seas, mists, dews, springs, even steam and ice;
Anaximander made the basic stuff
An abstract infinite, whence come all things,
Whither they return; Anaximenes, wise
In turn, claimed air or breath formed living beings;
Silly ideas, dispensing with the god,
Whence a new restlessness boiled in the blood.

V

Herakleitos denounced the mysteries
And thought the fairest universe a heap
Of rubbish fit for the fire; Xenophanes
Said God is not a donkey or a man,
That a new sun leaps daily from the deep;
Though Zeno thought swift as Achilles ran,
The tortoise of religion kept its lead
Because philosophy harangues the head.

VI

Pythagoras measured heaven's melody
On cords that any schooled ephebe might pluck
In Samos or in smoking Sicily;

His Hera in the ancient lyre-string measures
Confessed desire that mages fear to mock
Lest they become confused with white-armed pleasures;
Anacreon praised pleasure to the court
To salve a life that's brutal, mean, and short.

VII

Herodotus, returning to his theme,
Read Persia as a paradigm of pride;
As Croesus the drugged priestess named supreme,
So Darius and Xerxes. Histories
Repeat the common tragedy inside
The general that failed, Thucydides,
Who set the facts in selfless prose to teach
Us what the seawind teaches to the beach.

VIII

Zeuxis, famed for his Eros wreathed in rose,
To find the model for his Helen had
Croton's girls parade naked till he chose
The five most beautiful in every part
For a composite limned in light and shade;
He failed, until he plucked her from his heart;
But still it was sweet joyance to his eye
To see the naked maidens dancing by.

IX

Plato kicked out the poets - a wise move -
Who don't respect republics of the mind
When frenzied by the Muse or sick with love
Or twined in the entanglements of story,
Who know metre grows strict when unconfined
By moral law or pieties of glory;
But Aristotle really made them leery
By circumscribing poesy with theory.

X

The marble Aphrodites of the grove
Of fluted columns, crouching, turning their
Strong haunches in a posture meant to prove
The energies of a sublime repose
That animate the apple, fig, and pear,
Lifting their breasts as they let glide their clothes,
Give freely to all girls, highborn or slave,
An independence erotic to the grave.

XI

The islands and the shores in summer light,
The salt and wind from Homer's scary sea,
The daze of noon, the clarity of night
Where constellations seem to stay the same
And dazzle us with anonymity,
And the one word of tragedy and blame,

Though doomed, endure beyond our truest grief
And all the ironies of disbelief.

BIBLICAL QUESTIONS

Was Eve's fresh fruit an apple or a quince?
What lure of sweetness did her honeybees
Of April find, what nectar to convince
The hives of the frenzied dance?
What mortal man would dare not disobey
His winter's regimens for these?
The questions fuel the man, our sages say.

What disposition swirls the desert air
That Solomon forsakes his harem snoozes?
What unguents scent Queen Sheba's shining hair
Cascading by her ear
With blue stone flashes? What wisdom wanes forlorn
Where law is registered by ruses?
The questions fool the man, our sages warn.

When Judith lopped off Holofernes' head
Was that a lady's honest politics?
And was the corpse left thoughtless in the bed
Now dyed a richer red
A joke to his won wives? What troops could hurry
The logic of the lying sex?
The questions foil the man, our sages worry.

Eve proffers him her fruit that he must bite,
And Sheba's statecraft is the best of all,

And Judith needs more than an urgent night
Rightly to praise his might
And rule within herself his tribal rages.
What man, bemused and biblical,
Shouts questions at the dumb and distant sages?

PICKING CHERRIES AT HAGIOS IOANNES KAPAROS

"Each act bears fruit; beware,
My friend," he laughs. Inside, we drink
A glass of his raki; it's strangely pink,
But pure, potent, delicious. Sitting there,
We're loth to get
To work. "To work is wise
While it's still cool." His little gray-striped cat,
Unused to strangers' ways, runs as we rise.

Though early, it is hot;
Among the cherry-dripping trees
Cicadas, dinning louder than loud bees,
Ignore us, though the swellthroat birds do not
Who wait to see
Where we are going: Just
To pick sour cherries from the biggest tree
Where sunlight leafglows like an aureate dust.

We break the fibrous stems
As we're instructed, and we eat
A cherry every four or five; their meat
Is sour and firm; crimson as blood on gems,
Their red juice runs
Down our raised naked arms;
Even through laden boughs the shaded sun's
Heat makes us squint. Hawkcries are not the farm's.

Five pounds of cherries in
Our bag, and careful not to squash
Them they're so ripe, we climb the wall to wash
The sticky bloodstreaks from forearms and chin
At the old cool
Cistern that's filling from
The dry thyme-fragrant mountain; such renewal
Scares cistern frogs still in the insect-hum.

On hand-held scales he weighs
Our fruit and offhand drops the price.
"These are," I say, "the fruits of Paradise."
He nods with blithe forbearance. When he prays
To St. John's blessed
And wormy icon he
Asks the Forerunner not for wealth or rest
But for right winter rains for field and tree.

DEMETER'S TEMPLE, NAXOS

What dare we ask? A temple is a house,
Though twistier than a good woman has.
What can we ask? A woman has her reasons,

Whose manners shift, whose mind remains the same,
But unrevealed. For us her body is
The sign of knowledge, symbolizing grief;

For us her body, splendid in its foison, 's
The sign of longing, symbolizing chance.
We see the temple when we park our bike,

Check out the likely route and start to hike.
The path down alternates its flowers and thorns,
But is not so devious or risky as

A dawn's embrace, because a mystery
Is what we are graced with as the greenest way
To enrich the mind's confusion and confirm

Labor's sacredness and its mean constraints.
Grainlife and starlife, say those signs, are one,
Say faith in things is foolish or insane:

She opens her white arms to sun and rain.
An eagle grabs a rabbit, a hawk a mouse,
An owl a snake. Such mediation warns

That given images are female feints,
And there's no trust in mountain clefts and horns.
Her sacred dance sways to a belly dance

In which her belly is a mound of grain.
No wonder I am hot; the sun's a spike;
I shed my shirt, you open up your blouse.

The path's descending progress is not plain,
Winding through burning sun and shade's relief:
Of all her movements twisting is the chief.

Among her terraced fields, away from sea
Or Naxos town, her temple's stones still form
A mental map of land's fertility

To guide the wayward eye through starlit seasons
That measure life and death - ploughed soil, cold, warm
New shoots, stacked grain and burning yellow hay.

Nature's terrors that her dark grievings tame
Heap barley, wheat, oats, vetch, and sesame
As offerings displayed upon a tray.

Having climbed down, guided by her glance,
Past tended churches of her minion saints -
Byzantine rubble for a change of name -

To this ruined hillock (her ruins hide her fame),
We sit and rest, convinced by what we like
Or fear, and then her hymn's words start to swarm.

ARCHAIC

The gods rule earth and heaven in their own
Inscrutable interest, not at all in yours,
And if your life is short, and your strength feeble,
Your hopes doomed to be disappointed, and
Your health, life, friends, wealth, thought
Precarious, it does not signify
They disallow moments of happiness
Or aureate felicity. Since fleeting,
They are preserved in fleeting poetry
For you to speak and weep in ignorance.

And lusty enterprise requires no hope.

THE OWL

Aloof watches the owl
With wide indifferent eyes:
Life long in the foul,
Life short in the wise.

THE SWALLOWS OF THE VILLA ROSPIGLIOSI

All night under the wooden eaves
Day's raucous swallows sleep, each one
Two inches from his folded fellow
As swallow laws decree it done.
Wind in the olive-orchard leaves
And fruits, bass frogcroaks in the shallow
Pool's fat lily-platforms and folded flowers
Do not disturb the silence of their hours;

Dawn does. It chimes the villa's dull
Patchy ochre the same time as
It tinges the rich nurseries
Of Arno's plain with hue that has
An ancient summer in its pull
From stout Etruscan symmetries
The landscape's rules demand. Now one or two
Leap groggily off their ledge. Dull rest is through

For twelve bright hours on graceful wing
In Tuscan air. The sluggards follow
And in two minutes every bird
Is shrilling "swallow" "swallow" "swallow"
Ungathering and twittering
Till almost too high to be heard
Below, where we sit on the dewdrenched lawn
And wake to repetitions of the dawn.

The thinning flock yet lingers near
Its roost, hunting the moist half-dark's
Last insects the returning bats
Have not devoured. A pair of larks
Calls from hydrangaeas. Skirting where
We're sitting, two rotund farm cats
Head home. The swallows dip now in the sun
For insect meat, until flock-form is gone.

Their wings are long and pointed and
Their tails are forked; their flight is fast
And elegant; their legs and bills
Are short; their soaring joy can last
All day, disdaining flat farmed land;
Their throats are crimson; over hills
And plains and gray mediaeval towns they soar
Disdaining what Dante climbed from Hades for.

At dusk the tune's in retrograde
As flock-mates gather in the sky
A deep mosaic blue and green,
And we imagine that they fly
As restless as the men who made
Our mental canons here. They've seen
What we would give much to relearn aright.
Their quarrels cease; wings fold them into night.

NEL CAFFE

Out of the rain, I'm jostling in a Florentine caffè
Among the gleaming chrome, the shiny glassware, the rich smells
Of ground espresso beans, the flaky pastries, and the smart
Damp people furling drenched umbrellas; I can't catch what they say
In their bright tongue, my mind's too slow. The waiter's glare compels
A coffee, which no doubt I'll need in my long day of art,

An inquiry my friends consider dutiful and dry
When so prolonged. What do they know, who don't believe that paint
Is the pursuit of hidden knowledge and the order that
Is laid upon things like an invisible net? The inmost cry
Is for such beauty and such science, not the aesthetic quaint.
The rain goes on. I eat a pastry though I'm getting fat

On all this goodness; substantial as a Giotto, I'd like to think.
Are all philosophies of art and life "as if"? Perhaps.
But then why not seek out the architecture of the mind,
The abstract music that's sensual, in female flesh that's pink
With blood, in men's aplomb and muscle. True perspective traps
The thought in systematic webs. As if things were designed

In such a way that thought and conscious art could apprehend
The definite. As if gross nature were not an adequate
Subject, and skill more than the portion of the diligent
In talent. Now that the half-hour rain is coming to an end,

The caffè empties out. I cross the river and can't wait
To wonder once again what mind-driven Massaccio meant.

THREE TRAGIC POEMS

I O ONCE MORE

O once more
to be immersed in new fire
Scorched
by initial energy and desperate ignorance
Untouched
for the sake of lust
O to be verdant in gold mosaic fire
within a mandorla of lustful doves
cool cooing and hearts beating white down

But when the Woman Earth
wet with rain or dry with spices
in rivulets of cress and dill
mid thyme or heliochrysum ravines
touches the seasons all at once with fragrance
Then the naked girls with baskets of husked almonds
They take from Thetis when she is a shore mist
At dawn or dusk
hand you icons of themselves
the halved white husked almonds
all gold with
sea mist
a woman's salt

thou sayest opening thy morning robe
"You must not formulate this in abstractions
the stars are infinite but not abstract"
and every year thy mulberry tree has berries
some years many and fat some years few and dry
        but always berries
sparrows and warblers quarrel in the leaves
copulate among the leaves
the leaves are streaked with purple droppings
green thy gift and gone and green again

        but abstract is a way
        to make things parallel connect
        the Halo and the Woman
        the flamingo of the soul
        whose Halo is flaming into gold
        into eternal tesserae
        each tessera a forming star

Slate and rain and sandy wind
And all the hopeless writing of the bark
And poplar strips and torrents of the spring
Pine needles caught in rivulets of resin
Give us an order even though thy words
    "Better to know the names of flowers in the garden
    than of angels
    of course Angelico's are flowers"
    would frighten me if I knew what they meant

I'm frightened anyway the scary green

ὤμοι, πέπληγμαι καιρίαν πληγὴν ἔσω
I'm struck a mortal blow

ποντίων τε κυμάτων ἀνηριθμον γελάσμα
the sea's waves sparkling

We set white marble fountains in the streets
whose single eagle twines its noble heads
we build our churches abstract in the sun
with all the whitewash of our ancestors
our songs are lustful as birds
the sparrow cock sits on his post and flaps his wings
and when his hen flies in with grass he struts and sings

But when the fireball came across the sky
To show how much the night is really gold
From east to west in midnight's moonless sky
I didn't know what to ask
but when I discovered what I wanted
to ask old Aeschylus
he had left for Sicily
angry as Arethousa
and all we heard were preposterous stories
of eagles and turtles
and wind that fills the marble troughs
because heaven strikes the mortal blow

and when I said to thee
"One cannot know the peace of dawn or dusk
without the strength and mystery of noon"
the fire of mystery when all the colors merge
not only into white but gold of something else
then thou disrobeth in noon's privacy

The mandorla of night
the almond of the moon

There was a moment
smelling green as earth
when I could see thee fully
fear was not in such procession
and the abstract metres
filled with local melody
again the song of golden fire

And all the flowers bloomed with names
each flower a tessera
for me to learn again.

II THE FIRST SUNSET

That first sunset
over the yellow beach and the palm
the fields of heather a lake
the frogs brekekekex koax koax in fresh water

darting dragonflies and reeds
two meters from the sea that's dark
and gold
because the swallows are crazy with evening singing
and the cloud of insects rising and falling in the valley
and it is already colder than the pungent hillsides
May be a beginning
that reaches an end now
where I begin and start again all blue
because of daemons in the lemon trees
cicadas in the eucalyptus trees
who cannot be stopped from singing
carob trees orange trees quince trees
and hosts of invisible people to keep me company

Because I am alone with white chapels
Because I have a wife father mother brother
Because my friends do not love one another
three Black Fates
still as if after a dance
the first modes all Black
warn me

But who am I to heed
voluptuous but not enough
willing to praise with frogs and swallows
but not enough
while the clouds change color from copper to purple

On all Saints Peak they
will wait all night

πολλὰ τὰ δεινὰ
Many things

but Sophocles' gods have different wonders
keep away

The Evening Star flashes in her private way
So I shall dream of her till dawn
She likes to call me Adam call thee Eve
She is mocking thee and me
despite the golden orioles
despite the nightingales and blackbirds
βρεκεκὲκὲξ mock the happy frogs
and donkeys bray goats bleat cows low dogs bark
nymphs with no name no word for their allure
more erotic in the flickering

"I don't understand anything" we admit
least of all how the world
is written in me
but I cannot see in me the blue
thou cannot

But Evening herself is young and in love with color
Creating herself generously unswervingly who knows perhaps cruelly

and they say Sophocles died happy
sued by his son raving like Philoctetes
so tell me
the double ax
the bull's horns
all the shapes in a jumble
the flowers and naked women
dancing in a ring to Sophocles' goddess-song
the Black Fates
the colors on the mountain changing
from terrace to terrace

and the words in my heart perhaps I do not understand
never good at that language thy language
The sea olive-oil between floating islands
there is something I should say
what tell thou me
The sea is flickering with memories green hair starfish breasts cold eyes
there is something with the blue of opals tell me
All the constellations of the night
Move at once

something ordinary is invisible
something extraordinary is visible and blue
and when I turn my back inadvertently as always
the sunset lasts
a second
longer.

III ZENITH

Whence in the meridian
Come the bloody traces in the azure

"Bird you sing a sad song round
the rocky headlands of the sea"
And Euripides is a lonely man
trying to think and chant for me
mourn and celebrate for me

Irises in the garden loud with bees
Little wild irises on the mountain
loud with bees
Iris in the sky after the rain
As all the clouds dissolve into noon light

The hungry eagle hunts at noon
And all the songbirds cease their shrill delight

But nothing again
after the rain
nothing

there's nothing for it empty as you are
the world's gone crazy and you're not smart enough
for the goldfinches in the old pine
the tiny pinecones far from dropping

Looking at the empty sky
            for the sake of a possible good moment
                        a line not quite your own

A bunting on the wire
            two buntings
(A robin on that mowed lawn smelling so fresh
Mowed by hand with a rusty yellow mower
For two bucks
            two robins)

                        so fast so fast
                        despite the evenness of wingbeats

                        like dandelion fluff or a skimmed stone
                        sudden points of light in air
                        and the sea not far

For in its season the pomegranate's thick rind
            Persephone's death-fruit
Will split open and show you the whole world
                        the golden bands the ruby star
The whole world in scarlet
                        don't weep

Perhaps this is what is meant by "writing in blood"
            bloodred poppies in the greengold wheat
            her rosepink nipples on her round white breasts

(crimson cardinals after a seed in snow)
red-greaved Mars with the Gemini
trecento vermilion in a haze of flickering gold

Don't weep
at the beauty of this dusk
with maroon light
then emerald light over the black islands
Venus shining steady in the west
at the bellezza of this dawn
warm sun on the mountain fields
old goats playing in the wildflowers
Venus fading steady in the east

even though your suffering is nothing
and hardly matters even to you
don't weep
the punishment is now
both for the dullness of response
and sloth of execution
for the pleasance and
the easy poise of talent in the pretty word
so don't weep
for the secret evil you don't know
or for the one you do
sometimes
when the world's evil is on the airwaves
bouncing around the empty cosmos

Dandelion fluff floats on the airwaves
With angels from before the Common Era
    with their cinnabar eyes

        Euripides in Macedonia
        listens to the forest
        the strange sound of running water
        the charming misplaced quantity of metre

τι τὸ σοφὸν
What is wisdom

        the ideas stop
        before the hope for them

Among the barbarians everything is the same
Even presumption in such innocence

But
    small silver earrings
    on her naked ears
    thy little flushed ears
        the moment flashes

For a moment you remember
    like an eagle's glint at noon
        in the zenith
Iris fading into something else.

TWELVE ANIMALS

1. New York, 1962

Astor Place subway station. A long delay, waiting for the train. At last a grey dog comes running frantically in front of it. He is too terrified for the platform, or for the third rail. A man laughs. "That's me", he says.

2. New York, 1964

Greene Street. A cotamundi jumps out of a garbage can and burrows under my armpit. He is quivering with fear and cold. The owner, a sculptor, much later when I find him, thanks me indifferently.

3. Paros, 1965.

A pale dun cow is tied to a stake. Two 10-year old boys are throwing stones at her full udders; she lows with pain.

4. Paros, 1966

Town beach. A young cat limps along the sand. A 14-year old boy picks it up by the tail, twirls it, flings it into the sea; his father laughs.

5. Naxos, 1970

Noon, very hot. A farmer on a tiny donkey urges it on by jabbing a stick with a nail stuck on one end into a sore on its neck. With each jab, the donkey jerks his head as little as possible.

6. Fiesole, 1972

The paved ascent to San Francesco. Two boys on bicycles, with sticks, play hockey with a hedgehog, batting it back and forth as they ride.

7. Yerolimeno, 1973

The harbor café. Three men are laughing at a golden oriole, shot in the wing, they have put alive into the freezer with the frozen fish.

8. Cairo, 1975.

A camel falls near the Old City of the Christians. Its owner beats it with a stick as it dies.

9. Mykonos, 1976

Town beach. A huge sea turtle, nearly dead, washes up on the sand, between two fishing boats . A crowd gathers. A man goes up and kicks it in the head to show his courage. The crowd oohs at him.

10. Paris, 1977

Jardins de Luxembourg. A girl walks her hopping pet sparrow on a string pulled through its dull spread wing. Her father instructs her.

11. San Diego, 1979

Zoo. A polar bear, crazy with misery, bangs his head bloody against his compound's hot concrete walls. A woman throws him crackerjacks.

12. Paros, 1980

A small brown dog wanders among the loading trucks on the dock. A man, annoyed, heaves a sack of cement on its back, breaking it. "Life's tough," a waiting driver says to me.

GOAT

In a mountain field of wild golden barley
And crimson poppies, a field whose walls still stand,
Unfarmed for a hundred years, a lonely goat
Looked at me with mad interest.

This was
No accident, this was a crazy proof
Of my imagination. This was what
I had been hoping for throughout the queer,
Forgotten centuries.

A mountain daisy
Between its teeth, and pollen in its beard!

THE TEMPLE AND THE DOLPHIN

April - June, 1993

When the blue dolphin leaps,
The arc stays there for keeps.

BIRD

Hard to see but close,
an inkgrey bird leaves claw tracks
of Ionic script
on all our island's sands and soils.

His birdsong sparkles
legible in sunlight.

THE DOLPHIN

The sea, transparent, is reflecting nothing,
And every dolphin-shape is visible,
A precedent intelligibility.

In my little boat, the *Sappho,* white with a seablue stripe,
I go by the Parian Gates where the seafloor rises
And marine infinity lifts the green with other colors flowing.
On the high bare rocks are April's asphodels and chamomile
Smelling through the spume. Titanic clouds, each separate
In the sky blue as a Parthenon and shifting very slowly,
Move like the minds of master poets whom I have neglected
In reading and in verses, the lines I meant to memorize
But didn't. Again.
What day is today? How many years
Have I been circling round this isolated entrance way
As dawns and noons and dusks avoid my anguishes
And joys? How blue!
The dolphin of my stirred imagination
(It's real it's real! a voice not mine affirms from nowhere,
From the rock and waves, from distant music of the island's mountains, from the flowering
Seafloor, or maybe just the sunlight's concentration)
Ripples silver just beneath the slight wind-ruffle:

How can you say "I love you" when it doesn't solve

The Equations? The dolphin says
"Make silver of the sunlight and the wavelight";
The dolphin says "Prepare
A starting point which is this point
Of beauty and of ignorance,
Of dire inability, for after all it's yours;
The sky's Patriarchs for your sake revise their texts,
For your sake call their feral theology Nature,
Offer you a Future in the silver of the Past".
But Nature? Because you loved as a child the spring rains rushing
Down a hillside's gully with its clay and wild garlic,
Robins bathing in the clearer eddies,
Forgotten when not subtly interfused
Like light in water chromed by wind?

The *Sappho* with its old oars and weak motor
Sends a single wave
A single silver wave to the great rock
Where a dolphin, who appears and reappears
According to no plan I comprehend, follows with a turn;
And swallows leave their rockcliff nests at my approach
And cormorants stretch their long black necks
And gulls floating like toy boats in the lee stay unscreeching;
But a peregrine falcon swooping from a high nest calls
"Danger, this is not your delight, go back! go back
To shore where I hunt day by day
For rats and mice and snakes and little birds
And shift my flight for your daily deference,

For poise and even art";

Wingbeaten wind

Rushes by my ears until I cut the engine, dive
Into the lagoon between the Gates, and watch
The sunlight and seablue silvering my flesh, and I smile
The dolphin's blue smile for all
The schools of fish that turn from silver to invisible
To silverblue again:
"Invert every moment with a turn
So that the moment is eternal and
Eternity a flash of scales
From silver to invisible to silverblue again."

Returning to the *Sappho*, I shake the seadrops off,
Pass between the fragrant Gates
And head for Paros, bay and safe moorage.

PRELUDE

At the far point of Santa Maria headland
Birds sing the prelude to the morning service
In dark Poseidon's precinct, in pounded ruins
Of his temple - if it is Poseidon's,
For there is no inscription to the god
To prove what sense proclaims, what place demands,
On marbles marking out a firm foundation.
Yet who else on this high rough promontory,
Overlooking the Naxos straits whose currents
Drive black ships south too swiftly for strong oarsmen,
Would take surveillance here to see the sunrise
Over the massive peaks of Zeus's Naxos
Striping the straits with gold? Who'd wait for the words
Scared mariners cry out in desperate metres,
Promising a fat calf or white church
That clings to a seacliff like a crab to searock,
To Spyridon, Nicholas, or salty Sozon?
Among the shards and stones blue irises
Unfurl in April as winds blow from the south.
The flitting swarms of finches, warblers, swallows
Disdain all prayers in the morning light
And keep their shifting distance as I approach.

I've never met another person here,
Though goat-droppings are dark and goat-bells distant;
Who knows this temple's presence? It is on

No plan though its own plan is clear enough
Among the limy rubble, thorns, new spring flowers,
And wind-eroded shards with rubbed black glaze.
From splendid isolation the god communes
With Zeus, Apollo, Helios, Aphrodite
And St. Antonios on his columned peak,
All present in a natural blueprint
Whose precincts give geography to Paros
And Naxos in its close black might. I stoop
To pick up an obsidian arrowhead
Left by a hunter shooting at a hare
(I saw one in my early scramble up
The slope from Santa Maria beach) perhaps
Five thousand years ago, before the gods
Had names for me to gloss or knew my theories
Of where they'd best command a cynosure,
Nature's focus conducing to my own.

An eagle - they are not rare here - crosses from Naxos,
As if the straits were nothing, here to Paros,
After the same hare or just soaring on
The stiff interisland draughts. Augury,
It turns out, is no great trick, and any
Early man turns augur in such a place
Among the flowers fast losing their dew.
"Caw caw" say crows in a dwarf-cypress tree
At the precinct's indistinct edge, and then the songbirds
Start again their din of happiness

At things to do.

Their service in dawn song

Becomes a kore in the manly precinct,
With glinting pearls around her naked neck,
But birds and irises should have prevented
My dumb amazement. And as she glides among
The ruins Poseidon smiles, and I smile too
With pleasure at her comely verification.

Now that the sun has risen, the running strait,
Where Dionysus once turned greedy men
To dolphins and their mast to clustered vines,
Turns cyan-blue between its dazzling points
Of light. It is time for me to go back;
I have my normal day of griefs and pleasures,
Of passing time, the joy of thought, the hope
Of poetry, the residence of ruins,
A temple's fading in the stronger sunlight.

OXYRHYNCHUS

Boring lists of dates, the financial transactions
Of dull business men, of temples greedy
As ever, grammarians' ramblings, compilations
And synopses of sources secondhand
Even then when one could disbelieve
In gods one prayed in fear to, bit by bit
Emerge from a garbage pit of junked papyrus
Like a scarab beetle from a dungheap pushing
His dungball golden as the sun to him.
Ragged strips, scraps, scored and tattered rolls,
Hellenistic, Roman, bleak Byzantine,
In the rubbish dump of a half-known half-Greek city,
Indifferently debased and so spared by
Egyptian sand and random desiccation,
Make piquant items for our rich collectors,
Who relish preservation's new expense
And visits from professors with a grant.
And when some treatise on old metres yields
A line of Sappho or Archilochos
In quantities that no one can pronounce
So bright they are, some line-ends from a hymn,
A verse long edited out of the *Iliad*,
A few stray strophes of Sophocles, an entire
Scene of Menander Shakespeare would have stolen
Had he the drab confusion of our monied
Scholarship, an offhand fact decoding

Emotions we should certainly decry
If we again but knew them ours, an age
Unknowably chaotic as our own,
We're justified by scholarly conclusions.
"Nothing can be known." On the lone sands
The dust of the inevitable conflagration
That gobbled Alexandria's papyri
Uncovers the fragment - a line of verse, what else? -
That we await, and that we do not want.

PAROS MINOR

Between Naxos and Mykonos I have disclosed
An island with a house for us and a garden
Watered by a spring named for a nymph,
And called it *Paros Minor*. Though it is small
We could not learn its secrets in a lifetime
Or weep enough for any of its woes
Or keep a daybook filled with all its flora
Or its migrating birds that stop to rest,
To drink, to eat the grasses' snails and insects.
There's shade for summer sun and walls for winter,
A room for shuttered thinking, and a small
Olive grove for strolling in at dusk.
Here pleasure turns to joy and lust to love,
Perplexity to verse, and daily sadness
To abstract thought or rhyme. I have disclosed
That fantasy of bookish humanists,
A lover's isle, whose lovely shape is close
On clear days in our blue Aegean straits.

READING, 3:OO A.M.

Full moonlight streamed in through the bedroom windows,
And shadows in the room were not malignant,
Certainly no distraction from his book.
Even the moths' wings beating at the pane
For the unaccustomed light could be ignored
As he became his book, the world his book,
Unmotivated by the moonlight's beauty
Or thrashing of a tail in heaped dead leaves.
How can one hope to live within confusion
If one cannot experience the world
Through other eyes, escaping to return?
His eyes follow the words page after page,
An isolate of intimate relations.

DANAE'S DREAM

Danae's luscious thighs are opening stroke by stroke
To the golden shower of fertile love, divine
If anything is divine; she's longing for her fate and that's
What makes her beautiful and fills our red blood
With the desire of money soft to the bite.
Her jewels glimmer her worth and energy, and every
Coin is stamped with her likeness from the brazen doors.
Even the hag grabs the gold: yes, this is
Annunciation.
                    The sea
Will flower all the way to Seriphos,
And the witch's writhing head
Will blazon on the breast of Wisdom; beautiful. The gods,
Predicting Tragedy, praise us, and fathers
Who want an easy old age
Must get it otherwise in any case: discus
In the heel and no bright constellation.

"My fate is my desire" - how horrible! The hero
Looks away, advancing with his mirror and his sickle.
How horrible! He, at least, will not be happy;
He, at least, defeats the men of stone. And Danae
Covets this pleasure, not the next, the way a leaf
Surfs to its wavy edge.

Her mirror, polished bronze,
Shows Aphrodite in the selfsame pose. It's true,
Nature is prettier when we look at her,
She frets the dill and opens in her roses,
She needs us and is our concern. And if when we become
Golden constellations -
Abstractions in the beautiful night sky
That old men track with numbers and lovers with their sighs -
Still she was once a certain way, even in the gleaming Dungeon,
Even in the floating casket and the violence of soul.
Conception is irrevocable. She wore
His power and his knowledge just because of that,
Who certain things cannot surpass. The green leaf
Surfs to its wavy edge with pleasure's shudder.

"I limp like Perseus over the stones", but women,
It's known, *like* men who limp when wounded by the female earth,
Say wreaths of female myths and vanished poems
Of leaves and waves and proper husbandry.
The rivulet of syllables, the long
Lines, attempt the risk of life
Because at least mere life is utterable,
Because, despite the Tragedy - no, because of it -
It's worth it, like digging
In a garden after rain.

Heroes, living, are afraid,
And women, living, open luscious thighs
To them because of it. They praise their men,

Their children born to bawl and die. And they die
Of suffering that is too much to bear:
Digging in a garden opening to sunlight
To see what it will bear.

So much gold, more than we can spend;
So much pleasure, more than we can feel;
So much pain, more than we can damn;
So much suffering, more than we can rage against and praise.
And so? No matter. This is Danae's dream:
To be the naked Queen of every living thing,
Something ordinary as that, as storms and quiet after.
And what mere god could slake such vast desire?

HER HAWKS

Stand on the porch between the fluted columns; this
Is not where you entered from the winding path.
Go out the narthex not as you are, and as you are,
With your eyes on the undulating mountain clefts,
Turning on the Sacred Way - it's enough to imagine it
As your own Sacred Way with altars of reverence and awe
And stone stelae with carved unsettling distichs in old hexameters -
Toward the other line of mountains with its peaks and clefts,
Its groves and springs and dark ravines,
In the heat haze and the sea mist.

Hawks

Soar with a dip from one ridge to another,
And you, in the precinct in between, on a round bare hill
Measured by a parapet with fine reliefs of wind,
Are augur and all the auguries
Are rapturous with disbelief, complaint, and unsuccess.
Fear them, fear them, they bode nor well nor ill,
Despite the preparation of the temple,
Despite the frieze and volutes and fine mouldings
Of wind. Blue sky, red blood, and the interior glow
Through thin marble slabs. A honey cake or poem
Left for the dim cult statue in her painted chiton,
Over her fine strong figure and her symbols.
The swallows making mud nests in the overhang.
Incense of wind, prayer of wind. Azure wind.

Still the mind's afflatus; think a single thought
Clear as you can, then hold it, then think the next in sequence;
And if this is not poetry, it's poetry
For gods. Do not the anxious gods launch hawks on wind?
Does not the fertile valley wheel and demarcate
Its zodiac from where you stand moving your eyes?

Descend, and now the bird is watching you,
Fixing you as prey, her prey. Pray
Your twisting way down steps and paving stones
When each one of your steps makes something sacred,
Adjusts her pose, and fills the wind with pollen.

TO NOON

Noon, with your white shark's belly upturned in the sea,
With your white vulture's breast curved in the sky,
With your extreme echoes of white,
I take your measure with my foot on the threshold.
I count the points of dazzle and the trails of particles,
Disdain the fevers and the airy desiccations.
The small seabirds crisscross indignantly,
The schools of flashing fish withdraw their silver.

Language lapses. Noon, you are absolute
And featureless, deficient in the human enterprise
When there is no response that is adequate,
When there is no response. "I take your measure."
But there is nothing to measure, the measures are my heartbeat,
Like the numbers of the neutral instant
Of which I am the sole imagining force.

Infinities are suspect. Quantum fields
Are nothing in such intensity of absence,
Into what would they explode mere white?
The entrails spilled throughout our Century
Of slaughter and of tiny hates are nothing
Since unthinkable, are measureless
With lapsed humanity. Noon,
How could you cleanse such lapsing memory?
Why do you hold still as a sleeping bat?

Surely *you* can see the opposite stars
And hear the notes with clear articulation.
Even your ossuaries, all exposed,
Have purged themselves of myth and bleached all blemishes.
What age of gold lacks such a lineage of bones?

Into what other noon are you staring
With such blank concentration? I'll say a word,
Recall a word of comity and praise,
With my foot on the threshold,
Though there is nowhere that I do not trample you
As if you were the purple grapes on whitewash
Strengthened by a week in wrinkling sunlight,
Or wine in a sealed jar for a surge of years.

Noon, my shore when seen from sea goes flat and white,
The cochineal insects and the gamboge flowers
Mean nothing to your dilations in the rocks and cliffs,
The limestone and the granite. Perhaps your other noon
Is infinitesimal in the speechless stone,
All turbulence infolded, all pressure reversed.
Your way is limitless, your breath from elsewhere;
You do not confuse the living and the dead
Who move in you as single points of dazzle.

Your great fact is the Sun I dare not look at
(The eagle's eyes gaze down),
Who magnifies his energy to white

Like a boy with a glass and blade of grass,
A little curious and heedless. Conflagration.
But this my heart can beat to, conflagration,
Till all the fuel is gone and he's a glow,
Till he's a rock that shuts in mysteries of endless entropy.
Systole, systole, till the conflagration!

Well, noon, you are beating with my heartbeat,
Or tricked me till mine is beating with yours.
And yes,
The small seabirds crisscross with cries of pleasure,
The schools of fish relapse with flashing silver.

SIESTA

The town square is deserted.
The lion's mouth keeps dripping
Beneath a huge plane tree.
Girls in summer dresses
Lean out of curtained windows
Or stand in open doorways,
Cool as this year's wine
In shaded earthen jars.

SEABREEZE

Here's my beloved seacliff once again,
The bay where summer dawns I used to swim and fish,
The rock where winter noons I used to muse,
The surfbeat whence my heart's metres derive
As they derived a score of years ago.
The pools of salt; the flashing mica chips;
The seacave where kingfishers used to hover in the dark;
The offshore rocks where pygmy cormorants sit,
Their necks black question marks; the gulls that rest on water;
The headland's little church across the bay with its blue dome;
The white town clean at distance; the mountain where the sun
And moon rise with incantatory rhythms
Of the poem that I was meant to write but won't
Since slothful, broody, and a man
Who cannot shuck his age with an inward shrug,
Exhausted as his century, too old to start again,
And bored with repetition, helpless at shipwreck;
White pigeons lifting from a marble tray;
The putt-putt of a fishing boat's bad motor:
The grey reply is sunstruck as the green.

I could say, at least, I was wiser if only
I could attach a meaning to the word "wise".
No, not even then: the gods hate hubris.
"The wise seabreeze", now that makes sense!
But man? The seasweet beauty is the same.

After so much desiring, no wonder the flesh grows old.
Or yet it is a wonder, yea a miracle of freshness,
Freshness elsewhere, a seabreeze on your shoulders.
Who loves his wrinkles and the patient threat,
No, not Death's commonplace, religious entropy,
But simply all the effort of desire
That needs a different tending?
                                        La chair est triste,
The flesh is sad, since first
The seabreeze smooths it, then toughens it for life,
Then leaches floral bloom like bitterness from purple aubergines.
Preserve yourself with oily anodynes,
Screen off the damages of sea and sky and earth,
Rely on constituents not of the Elements:
The hucksters tempt you, probably they are right,
As if your best were a fragile epigone,
A mix of what you were and could have been.
But sun and wind and sea again
Are wine and bread and Kore.
Your flesh takes on an hour, your thought takes on a year.
If you cannot remove the heavy half
Out of old skin in time then you are doomed
To be a painted crone whose teeth smell bad
And not the scary visage of the seafloor,
A countenance that keeps the crows indignant.
No, not doomed, that must be wrong, for you're doomed anyway
Since no one fools a soul, and Death
Is anorectic and unsensual,

Suspicious that all nourishment is adulterated,
All condiment mere rottenness preserved.

So as the wrinkles written with your failures
(But written in the metres of success)
Incised with acid of sad humanity,
Grow more and deeper, let
The seabreeze freshen absolutes,
Inverting like sky shining itself back through sea,
Obverse and reverse,
Like flipping coins to show their symbols:
Dolphin and Ear of Wheat,
Owl and Eagle,
Kouros and Kore,
Horse and Inked Reed Stylus,
Whose want requires a fruitful withering.

But here's the salt seabreeze now from the north
That cools these coasts as the sun ascends
And fringes the shore with feminine stitchery
And raises colors of last winter's rainbows
In the shallows with their seaweed, sea-anemones,
And boulders rough with barnacles or slick with seamoss.
And silver waves from fishing boats returning
Before the rising wind whips up the world.

ARION AND THE DOLPHIN

In lyric, dithyramb, and chantey life is hard,
But no escape that functions leaves life out.
So rail, Archilochos, rail, for we -
Despite the angry wasps around your marble stele
(The stele gone from the Elitas riverbed
but the wasps still there),
Your cow-lyre that made "iamb" into "I am",
Your lovely lies and love,
your sweet and stinging rage -
Can make what we will of you, in our own measures.
"O how I long to touch
Neoboule's hand".
Oh how I long, on seaside,
To feel the down on Aphrodite's flesh,
With lily fragrance and the offshore dolphin.
Saint Aphrodite, visit us! between
Wave and wind, wind and wave.

Friend, visit your dead, and then educe your forms:
Your boulder in the seasurf where the gulls dry their feathers,
black sea-urchins, the girls with ribbons,
and the briny smell;
Galatea on her water wheel,
Sea nymphs and satyrs praising her with lithe concupiscence,
copulate in the foam;
The cave of mysteries glinting with metal.

Let Proteus educe his forms from flux
To keep the fish amused,
And Triton blow his wreathed horn, and Neptune learn his Greek
Because the dead do not lie quiet but
Require the singing blood of effort and sea-reverie.
At water's edge, fast swifts
Swerve, swooping after dragonflies,
Their black wings almost dipping in the sea,
                dipping in Aphrodite's foam.
Marble pebbles make a pavement
                white and black and green
For a mermaid's naos or an octopus's.

Arion needs a lyre of ivory and gold
For orgies of the dithyramb and clarities of lyric,
Who made the dithyramb say "I am" and sing the world
To Aphrodite in Corinth, to Dionysos in Sicily.
The sailors want his money, the sea is hard,
They have not supped in the megara of tyrants
Or worn such fancy clothes, drunk honeyed wine.
The Lesbian poet's prizes are too rich.
"Jump overboard, or kill yourself
If you want a barrow on the shore.
No escape." "One last song, a chantey."
He puts on his fancy singing robes, tunes his lyre,
Sings amidships to the greedy sailors,
And finishing before their wits return,
Leaps in the dark sea in his precious robes,

clutching his priceless lyre.
The sailors get their money, a lively tune to boot,
The ship sails on to Corinth, they divvy up the loot,
Less than they had hoped, not worth the tyrant's wrath
Who keeps fine singers at his court; they are doomed.

But *Arion and the Dolphin*? What music crept by him?
A family of dolphins with their pups
Sees gold and ivory,
A drowning man in rich embroidered robes
To whom the strains of song still cling like seaweed.
The sea is calm, the surface breaking silver
With their every breath. They circle him, he's gasping.
A bluegrey dolphin proffers him a fin,
Swims Arion to Taineron, the rocky cape, to hallowed ground
And leaves him on the dolphin-smiling curve of beach.
Arion is alive, the dolphins care for music.
He wins more prizes, sets up a small bronze dolphin,
a man riding a dolphin,
In the temple which must still be there.

After our day on Mani
We took a fishing boat
To Matapan that once was Taineron,
And there were dolphins. Had a swim,
Returned, and there were dolphins.
And in my notes, this entry:
"The dolphins in our wake

Remember Arion, a legend for them too
In their most solemn Histories."
The temple then must still be there.

Educing form from flux, a fish
                    jumps and jumps again,
A school of fish, long and silver with blue stripes,
                    iridescent.
I plunge into the sea for my noon swim,
An hour of voluptuous escape,
And rising, open my eyes underwater,
Seeking dolphins, or the sunlit shade of dolphins,
A thing not impossible. And in
The little wake of foam I leave behind me
Are Amphitrite and Tyro,
                    Leucothea with her saltwhite cloth,
To apportion me the measures that I am.
Life is hard. "Stood on edge mid wave and wind".
So my old forms are here, my blood is singing
The dithyramb that dolphins love the best.

KORE'S LITTLE POMEGRANATE TREE

The pretty little pomegranate tree
We planted near our house's watered garden,
A twig five years ago in rocky soil,
Is blooming now with her red-orange flowers
Spaced like rhymes among the lustrous leaves.

The tiny grey Sardinian warblers, who
Tame with confidence hang on here all year
Varying their clicked messages like clouds,
Love her and flit in day's cool hours among
Sharp-pointed boughs and tiny leaves, repeating
Spring's sexy and assertive song, though they
Are hardly bigger than the flaming flowers.

The stories say her fruit is luscious death,
The stories call her seeds the bloody fruit
Of life, that newly crowned Persephone
Nibbled in Hades' gloom for their ruby glow,
And when her mother Earth rewelcomed her,
After the hymn's eternity of weeping,
To an embrace of grain and tears, she smiled,
Remembering the daisies she had gathered
While warblers clicked about her in the meadow.
Thick rinds, dull red flecked with autumn gold,
Burst and drip red seeds on autumn earth.

So Kore, pretty Kore then, who wreathes
The naked boy with tassles from ripe grain
In the Mysteries of flower, leaf, and fruit
Whose liturgies are silent till the end,
Of April's rain and August's burning barren,
Of butterflies and sun-maddened cicadas,
Bestows on us her fruit of quality,
Red seeds, red juice, stain of etesian blood.

THE WELL OF JOY

That week in April we were so filled with joy
Even the songbirds were attentive to us.

It was not something that we had to notice:
Our friends away, acquaintances forgotten,
A lull in mail, our farmer neighbors busy,
Our minds in focus shiny as the stars,
Our eyes in focus shining as the green
Marble pebbles in the thin freezing surf,
Our moments flourishing as vines and grasses
And heliotropic as the mountain's flowers.

It was as if the ants who reemerge
To carry off spilt crumbs and leaves and grain,
The grey crows who pick clean the carrion,
The turtles barging through the tangled weeds
Opening ways with headlong peacefulness,
The hermit crabs patrolling their white border,
Had made short work of ancient anguishes
And daily distress.

Why not: A nymph and faun -
At morning chores after a night of rain,
The smell of wet earth and dissolving clouds
In sunlight whose new strength pulses with growth -
Whom Erotes with short chromatic wings

Throng round with sudden curiosity,
As if we were the sculptures on a wellhead.

But Aeschylus says suffering is wisdom;
He's right, of course. And this is the same thing,
This scintillation of a drudgery,
This engine that will hum as long we do,
This nymph who suddenly leaps into her tree,
This well of joy to draw cold buckets from.

THE OLIVE GROVE

The owl in the olive grove
Hoots at my doubting, hoots at snakes,
Hoots for pleasure, hoots for love.
The sun has sunk over the glaucous sea,
withdrawn his golden ladder,
And shows Siphnos flat black and musical.
Chromatic splendor between there and Paros
Distills the last of spring flowers,
That cruel assurance of the life to come.

The plain fact is, more than halfway through life,
I am supposed to have some money in the bank,
Medical insurance, a car, a decent piano,
And to give some sums to worthy charities.
What a hoot!
And what if I don't deserve it?
"O the sun and the sea,
O the sea and the sun."
And women love money more than they love verses,
They've families and old age to attend to;
Pitched rhythms suit a young man,
too dapper and confused for prose,
Before a thought corrects his sentiments.
Who gives a hoot for an olive's obolus?

My neighbor's peacocks scream "paon paon"

too gaudy for sweet song
And go to sleep,
Penned lambs bleat for their grazing mothers,
Cows low to be milked.
The olivaceous warblers cease their song
Now there's no need of shade
And bees stop buzzing at the tiny flowers,
the seawind ceases.
The owl's song pierces rosy dusk
From olive treetop or found coin,
Familiar in the olive grove.
Owl γλαῦξ
glaux
Swoops from one olive tree to another
in last light
From one coin to another,
"such inadequacy!"

She stood beside me but I did not know her
Though far from home and desperate,
A shepherd girl who turned into a bird
After she gave her wise directions.
No shepherd girl
Has eyes that grey or stands so straight,
γλαυκῶπις
glaukopis (ops, eye),
A "virgin" with a past
Who loves the olive grove.

The olive leaves at dusk darken the silver
                    of their underleaves,
And then the owl-eyed maiden,
An olive tree, the olive tree she offered,
Whose best fruit is sweet
                    but bitter at the pit,
Stands in a tholos of shade,
                    the moon and vesper rising,
Oil for the civilized man,
                    gnarled boles for permanence,
Athena in the olive grove,
Hagia Sophia in the olive grove,
The owl hooting to her coded icons,
The cruel assurance of the life to come,
Plain facts:
                    Her Parthenon,
                    Her Church of Holy Wisdom,
                    The olive grove I'm standing in at dusk,
Owls in olive groves throughout the ancient valley.

SHIPWRECKED BY LIFE THERE IS MUCH TO SEE

Shipwrecked by life there is much for us to see:
Deep sandribs slightly different each day
Like flutings on strewn drums; changing sunsets;
Green mermaids sleeping on a wavy bed
Of sea anemones till tiny fish
Nibble their pale nipples and waken them;
Fluffed sponges clinging; distant shipwrecked sails
Sewn from the flags of tribes or towns or countries;
A swordfish leaping in a silver flash;
An octopus splitting muscular bivalves;
Bluegreen algae like an artist's outline
On the jagged rocks of unattainable coves;
Flotsam of war's lengthy prosperity
Becoming pure as crystals in the brine;
Sparkling phosphorescence when the moon
Is at the dark flickering flickering her halo;
A myriad of Sirens versing their visions
Proleptic or voluptuous; blue dolphins;
Constellations altering their pictures;
Forgotten ruins frightful to behold;
Bubble-swarms of baby jellyfishes;
Seabirds for whom the land holds no such promise.
There is much to see even in flung foam,
And nowhere else to see it but from here,
This spar of shipwreck, Leucothea's wind,
The memories more ruined than the world.

GOODS

Dingy as an island port in winter,
Lines creep across the smudged page,
Furrows on the brow.
The broken-down caique
Hauls real goods in its smelly hold,
Useful, not expensive.

MUNICIPAL GARDEN

Ah, among the watered plots of the municipal gardens
The hum of bees admires the usefulness,
The butterflies the order and the ease,
The birds the midday shade and trees
For quarreling before folding for sleep
Among the intricate boughs. How quiet!
And in the central row of dark green cypresses
The voices of the day rest in the umbra
Between the glaring harshnesses of sea and mountain,
Protected from the jumble of our lives and ways,
The rude possession of our anxious breathing and
The greedy town's fits and starts of action and destruction.
Wolves and lions leap among the deer,
How sad, how sad!
And life is limpid in the alternations
Of sun and shade, light like life
Whose channels follow irrigation runnels.
Green leaf, black bole, bright flower:
No, things are not only endless stones to dig
And stack into walls of futile demarcation.
The peristyle of cypress trunks, the ornamented lime trees,
The frieze of rosebeds and of myrtle,
The corner-mounted antefixes of bougainvillaea:
Ah, among the fragrant architecture
There must be words sleeping like birds,
Words for immutable desire that sing before they flee.

Wolves and lions leap among the deer,

How sad, how sad!

A MOMENT

"A god-touched glory", Pindar sang for supper
Of one of his forgotten wreathèd athletes,
"Shines a bright light on us and makes life sweet."
Does it? It lasts a moment,
And yes, it must be worth all the unfeeling hours.
The sun's face is hard, the moon's face is hard,
Indifferent to inadequacy; stars shine;
The pressure of fatality keeps changing
The poet's frightening astrology.

Such sweetness is the hope of "radiant poetry"
Whose making, Pindar exults, "is not easy."
But what if your most felicitous lines
Are not caught in the planet's lines of force
Streaming from white pole to pole?
Yes, when your lovely woman is most wanting it
You may or may not find your voice,
At the moment when its being is needed,
The moment of radiant love that needs a voice.

Or even, yes, the moment
When the goats come down the hillside -
Their kids bleating, their bells silencing
The crows in twisted dwarf-cypress trees -
To browse some newfound patch of thistles and flowering brush
In the cool of the day when the sharp wind recedes,

Yes, even that moment, in its changing radiance,
Before diffusing like day's cloud in bronze,
Needs silent wreathings of the heart's green voices.

DRIZZLE

It is perfectly easy to converse
With a goat.
You talk, she bleats.
It is winter, and the grass is rich,
But she is wet and cold and alone,
Her wet tether rubs her thin legs.

It seems we are discussing sorrow,
And sorrow is an eternal bleating
Hard to share, even with a goat.
But sometimes affinity comes easy,
And despite our isolation,
We listen to each other,
In the drizzle generous at last.

Her sodden coat is white with reddish patches,
Her female horns are small
On her daedalic head.

When she stops to eat
A swathe of new green vetch,
I leave, full of her complaints,
All true.

One voice in the drizzle does not vary.

WHITEWASH

Not even heat-haze dims the bluing's whitewash
In high July of the Cycladic round,
And all the sculpted statues have been burned
In limepits smoking just behind the beach
For whitening the islands modestly;
The statues' gestures are defined in light,
In which are struck the essential ratios.
The vacant temples now bare marred foundations,
Their dressed stones carted off for peasant houses
Or villas of the lucky rich where they
Cannot pose equally to ennoble slaves,
And flowering weeds have claimed the crevices.
The places where they stood are eloquent
Because of the inscriptions they obey.
When during the vexed Christian night the gods
Enwrapped their splendor from our place and prayers,
Enwrapped their simple beauty from our thoughts,
Then they became more truly what they are,
Invisible to mystics of the mind
For whom the ratios, though not believed,
Are images whose obverse is abstraction.
So when we love Ionic rhyme, the land
That flowers back into our memory,
Or blazing noon in high July, we love
Their potency of image that contrives
The ratios among sky, sea, and earth,

That hidden tone of reckonings approaching
Their desecration on white walls of stone,
And wring quintessence from our disbelief.

THE ICON

1993-1996

LARK

At dawn a lark starts singing,
Stops, starts even more clearly.

Do not reserve your simplest tunes
For verses in a room.
Even the lark at dawn does not.

The birds who sing themselves
Do not sing of themselves.
This is no paradox.

His crest is up,
His wayward flight exposed.

OVID'S BOOK

Of Ovid's characters half
Looked upon the divine mien,
Breaking a law forbidden
The waking mind. They all changed
For the worse, and subsided
Into something else.
                    Then did
Metamorphosis mean death
For him, his great book a book
Of flamboyant death? Yes.
                        But
Poetry provides the one
Method, its accountable
Craft, that's counting every breath.

OCCASIONS

On the few unexpected occasions
He was able to look into himself
He found cowardice, sordidness, moral deception.

He could never understand
How sometimes he could sing
Something more than himself.

ALEXANDRIAS

All these dead Alexandrias
Like footsteps in the lost Levant,
The toe more impressed than the heel:
The print of Alexander leaving
On his bloody trail of madness
To pseudo-Hellenize the world.
The heel came later. Deeper too.

PHOENIX

That's where the single phoenix hovers,
A blue point a mile up,
Where all the Parthenon's columns
And their twenty white flutings
Meet in a single point,
And it beats its wings so fast
For the sake of the music they make.

THE OLD APRICOT TREE

Three terraces above the house
in an untended field of grapevines
next to a huge boulder
jutting out from the crumbling cliff

an old
apricot tree

abandoned all these years
sparse
unpruned
unwatered

puts out five or six small fruits a spring.

The owner of the field, an old man,
most years makes it up to get them,
so, at their moment of perfection,
I only steal half.

They are
the best apricots I've ever had,
firm, with concentrated flavor.

And as for the theft,

some things are worth

the risk of personal honor.

ALEXANDRIANS

For as you have laid waste to your life here,
in this small corner, so you have ruined it in the whole world.
--Cavafy, "The City"

We too are Alexandrians, we too
Can salvage shards of strength from ruins we
Could not rebuild. The lovely surfaces
Of physics and of metaphysics still
Reflect each other's decorative abstractions
Whether our metrics deem them true or not.
We burn the scented midnight oil for joy
Of studying the obscure texts of our
Oblivion; and there is always love
And in decrepitude its memory.
The loss of our collective honor is
By no means loss of everything of worth.

BRIEF

Here on land the sea
Gives you buoyancy

And in the buoyant sea
You grasp the swaying tree

GLAUCOUS

Glaucous waves in daylight
Glaucous waves in starlight -
Are there Elysian asphodels
Under water in the daylight
Under glaucous water in the starlight?
Asphodels are tough and wild
                    weeds to farmers
With bulbs the starving man can eat

But aren't we all kith of Zeus?

The clouds are gathered and their aimed shadows
Make glaucous patches on the sea in daylight
Make glaucous portents on the sea in starlight
Homer's dreams recirculate to fashion something finished
A blue beginning with a glaucous past
All the sweet and vicious lies
The flattering stories
The personal despair of sordidness

Then even my troubles are sacred
Are soil for the weed of asphodel

A glaucous icon of Elysium
In whose fields the high mimetic heroes
Await you in an arrangement you are not exactly meant to enter

Is buried in a ruin of forgotten liturgies
Echoing the mountains and the shore
So that they are enhanced and thus completed

For whose few scattered marbles is no interpretation

The icon will save you if you find it
And you can only find it when the god
Sends you a dream
                of glaucous waves in sunlight
                of glaucous waves in starlight
And there on land is the goat that chews the thyme
And there in sea is the dolphin of silver thinking
And there in air are the falcons and the swallows
Guarding their nests on crags the wind has shaped
And bees with fresh pollen-loaves

The icon's encaustic burns!

No purity in nakedness
Oh youth's memory weighs you down as much as age
Perhaps is age
Immortal intimations as much as stupidity
And no solace in the light in water
The glaucous flash of jumping fish

Then even my troubles are sacred
Are soil for the weed of asphodel

That the center is where you stand
Is unbearable
But for the glaucous waves
And waves of wind and water
So start surveyance
Here
Right here where the wild hyacinth grows
Is trampled to a purple stain
And grows again next year
After dew and rain
In the seasalt air the
                    glaucescence

SEASLOPE

We're standing on green hills. Again it seems
The sea-horizon slopes down. A tilt of earth?
An illusion? Yet it is exactly here
The sun rises yolk-yellow. Then wait. Hold on.
White cocks are crowing in the freezing foam.

ACHILLES

Torrents or shooting-stars,
Heroes are men of no destiny and no anonymity.
We say the gods love them,
But the gods do not love anybody.
No, they are men of blood, performing their rage and their prowess.
And in the slaughter you can hear their blood vaunting.
Their great names are inscribed in the Annals of Honor
This very moment, then it's too late.
And the earth pulls its crooked magnetism.
So Hector fights mostly for wife and for city
And Odysseus fights to get home by hook or crook
And slyly fades from the picture,
And Aeneus has a dour destiny in time.

But there is no use for Achilles
Whom death polishes most brightly.
Lily of spring, he cares not for spring;
Flower of men, he care not for men;
Life hardly tempts him
Who suckled Thetis' foamy white breasts;
The lives of other men, the army's Ajax and Odysseus,
Hardly exist for him,
Except as formalities, rivals, or victims,
Lambs or lions to slaughter.
He could not exist without danger,
For well as he plays the lyre, what to sing but himself?

He fills hexameters' brim with the thrill of the bloodrush and godpull,
And the exquisite manners and enchanting girl-looks
Are to give poignancy to rage.

No wonder we love him who gilds
Our dark destinies with his deeds.
Because in his eagle-flight he soars
Briefly above his knowledge, his truly terrible knowledge
That the glorious arc of his flight
Is beautiful and useless and doomed,
That his future is the rainbow's,
That happiness is not to be thought of, a low if impossible thing,
Nor women beyond brief pleasure
Which may strengthen him or unstring him,
Nor orchard fruit-trees beyond a single flowering
That shakes in wind more fragrantly
Than soil and water can nourish.

And the obsession, the exploit, the blood
That soaks the furrows and stones,
So much blood the clear-flowing river
Reddens and turns against bloodrage,
These will be changed by us in a minute,
After he fades to a bloodless ghost,
Pallid to the furrow,
Into our pretty stories, our blithe hexameters,
That could never, as we know and do not care,

Have been true or even exact,

Except in the pure legend of wind.

THE CITY

[*May 30, 1453*]

Mehmet II the strong, son of Murad IV
(Who won much by his wise diplomacy),
Enters the City in state at last, the City
That makes him the one Emperor, makes him more
Than a Turkish Sultan and the vigorous scion of Osman,
With a taste for conquest, a taste for boys,
A taste for gracious overlordship
Of the tiles and carpets of his vast dominions.
No fortifications were stronger, no seat more enduring;
Arabs, Hungarians, Serbs,
Their tribute will have its significance here.
His doctor, a Jew, fired his longing for science;
A Hungarian forged the huge cannon
That battered the City's ancient walls;
A Venetian, the elder Bellini brother,
Will paint his delicate portrait with an Asian line;
And the Italian ships out-trade him,
Outfight him every time; and he admires them.
But his army is the best,
The biggest, the richest, the best-trained,
His faith the freshest, his tribe the fiercest.
Nowhere to go but outward. Marmara, Euxine, Golden Horn.
He feels about his fractious Greeks
As the old Italians did: they are good at art and philosophy,
Their tradition is the finest, their buildings the most prepossessing,

As soldiers, brave and tenacious,
But with an inner weakness in faction and in action.
He has studied their language and admired;
Their City is his seat at last, that had
A million people in its day
When his own ancestors were squabbling tribes.
But Latin freebooters, and plagues, and wars, and defection
Have left him perhaps 40,000;
Holy Wisdom is his, though the doors lie on the ground
And the light on marble and glass has grown dingy;
The great churches despoiled by his rampaging troops
And the heavenly mosaics blasphemous to his creed;
The palace in ruins, where the emperors rose enthroned;
The boys and women raped, enslaved, and fled;
The Hippodrome with its famous statues
Stolen by centuries of emperors to glorify it
When such things were the essence of Greek,
Has long lain in ruins of blue and green;
The columns fell before the gates were breached;
Fruit trees flower among the scattered stones;
Owls in their crumbling stone niches cry at night;
And as for the renowned scholars
With their precious books underarm
In the Greek of their ancestors
And their own unreadable commentaries,
Of Homer and Sophocles, of Archilochos and Pindar,
Of Plato and Aristotle, of Herodotus and Thucydides,
Of Hippocrates and Galen, of Euclid and Ptolemy,

Names a millennium old -
They have found cushy professorships
In the young Italian cities
Where Greek philology is the fashion.
He does not know these are the new Greeks.
He does not know, ambitious as he is
To be Emperor of Asia and of Europe,
That he does not have Constantinople,
Does not have the City, but something else,
Istanbul, great to be sure, but something else,
Constantine Paleologus vanished into the soil
And the Atlantic ocean forty years away.
Mehmet the conqueror is twenty-one years old,
Resolute and energetic and keen-minded,
And the unconquerable City of the Greeks
Has eluded him forever.

SPARROWHAWK

Sparrowhawk
On the wire,
How we gawk
At thy fire!

HIS BOOK

I've read my book,
And I'm a crook.
My straining verses
Earn my curses.
And my poor heart?
Wrong from the start.
The seed I scratch
Can never hatch.
A word or two
Just might be true.
Thus dull and trite?
Shut up and write.

OUR LATEST FESTIVAL'S MOST GRACIOUS LADY

Helen and Penelope, Grown Old, by Hera's Altar

PENELOPE. Well met in Argos' ancient precinct. Here
The crimson poppies raise their seeded rings
Betrothing color to the coming days,
And all the guests flash finery. The years
Are brief, the journey hard.

HELEN. Yet here we are,
Resting beneath a time-gnarled laurel tree,
Grandmothers old and wrinkled, pouched and pinched,
Dim-eyed and stooped and low-voiced, with frizzy hair,
My gold gone gray, your brunette gray, that used to flow
Below our waists, that we wove daisies in
When we were girls and pearls and golden bees
When we were the first ladies of our world
Of cities, palaces, and ships. And yet
We still are both accounted beautiful
As statues for the festival of Hera.

PENELOPE. Our image in her aspects. Let us rest.

HELEN. Tell me, what do you think men see who say
We still are beautiful? A veil of fame,
Like mist a goddess wears when half in sight?
The purling syllables of swirling legend?

And tell me, would you rather be a queen
Whose beauty sparks to everyone, or be
The mistress of some god or shepherd boy?

PENELOPE. Still thinking of lovers! Hera in a meadow!
What love or passion can there be between
A woman and an image? And shepherd boys
Remain available.

HELEN. Propriety
And circumspection are your legend's crest;
What chasteness in this jest of shepherd boys?

PENELOPE. You wrote experience upon the world,
But that does not mean I have none, who had
A herd of suitors waiting at my gate.

HELEN. They wanted money.

PENELOPE. They wanted money, true,
And they wanted me; my beauty, though not Leda's,
Was still ascendant then. But I kept both
My money and my heart for my husband's store.

HELEN. Our Hera in the myths of heroines!
No lover for twenty years! No wonder you
Stayed young in face and figure for so long.

PENELOPE. What makes you think I had no lovers?

HELEN. But
Wouldn't wily Odysseus have heard? There are
No secrets round the hearthstone of a king
As I know to my cost. Perhaps you've known
As many pleasures of the fragrant bed
As I? This thought is new.

PENELOPE. You never cared
What people said. My husband, the most clever
And keen of the Achaeans, never asked.
He probed into my heart, my proud desire,
And saw the woman that I really was.
Like you I did not care for common talk,
But cared for his return. The gods say we
Must have a husband, and I chose the best
From all the suitors in my father's hall,
Nor rich nor powerful, who would not leave
His home for the rich prominence of mine,
Who was my mate in wit and liveliness.

HELEN. How proper? You were famed for wiles and snares,
Famed for your grace descending palace stairs.
You trod conventions like the purple carpet
That Agamemnon strode on to his bath.

PENELOPE. Had I cared for my kingdom as I should
I would have married one of the wealthy princes,
As you did and your sister did, which drove
You both into extravagance and folly.
Had I cared for his poor land as I should,
I would have married one of the silly princes,
And not unravelled weaving or feigned weakness.

HELEN. It's true he made a woman know herself.
Athena was with him as Aphrodite
With Paris, who loved me more than the war,
Whom my husband could not beat, who slew Achilles.

PENELOPE. They both looked on a goddess' naked flesh
And did not die but grew more virile still.
He took no concubine on the plains of Troy;
For trophy he took agèd Hecuba
Agèd as we are now; Nausicaa
He left a virgin. There is not a woman
Who knowing him did not desire him too,
Not witch or nymph or goddess. You yourself -
Amid the opulence of your Trojan chamber,
The bright-dyed wool, the bronze, the furniture
Inlaid with scenes of women like yourself,
The painted pots and jewelry from Crete,
Translucent cloth from Egypt, embroideries,
Carved stones from craftsmen of the rivers' cities,
Things I could never possess on Ithaca,

A land of goats and rocks and terraces,
Far from the sealanes of Achaean ships,
Far from the markets of long-settled states
Where what is female still receives its due
In life and ritual - yes, you yourself
Did not reveal him to your charmed and dozing
Trojan guards.

HELEN. Whom else had I to talk to?
When I saw then he kept you always in mind,
I made no effort to deploy my charm,
Which wouldn't have worked. Though Paris also was
A woman's man and not vainglorious,
He lacked Odysseus' brazen gleam of mind,
And Hector had no curiosity,
And Priam was a father, not a lover.
No wonder Odysseus, whose brain and brawn alone
Could make a closure, was no tent companion
To men who vaunted most their reputations.

PENELOPE. You, married to a vain and foolish lord
For money and the exercise of power,
Ran off with the most beautiful of men,
A prince who, as you say, loved women rightly,
And no one blames you, neither man nor wife.

HELEN. Nor do I blame myself.

PENELOPE. For even I,

A woman blessed in husband and in son,
Envy you, who have met the world, have seen
The Cretan priestesses in drunken dance
With bare rouged breasts, have compassed polities
Where epos is inscribed on clay to read,
Where kings build tombs as mountains in the sand,
Where strangers of all garb commingle and
Where you were admired for what you really are.

HELEN. Yes, it is true. Had I Odysseus then
I would think I'd had all a woman wants.

PENELOPE. Hmm, "all a woman wants." My bones are tired
With longing and with waiting and with loving.
But, Helen, that is no concern of men:
We're wanted at the festival to sing
The praises of our Lady Hera. How do
I look?

HELEN. Like Hera.

PENELOPE. Helen of Troy, you look
Like Hera, mistress of the world's desire.

HELEN. We must sing them the hymn they need the most.
Old lady, let's go, and hold on to each other
For the paving stones are rough on this worn path

On which the poppies leave their sudden stain.

HYMN TO HERA

I sing of Rhea's daughter, white-armed Hera,
Who's seated on her throne of golden chasing,
Goddess and Queen of the most excellent beauty,
Woman to Zeus who wields the dinning thunder.
Achaean men and woman all revere her
As she descends to us in golden sandals,
Our latest festival's most gracious Lady,
Without whose benison our hearts would wither.

"THE CHORDS, THE CHORDS"

What to say to a master?
Gathering a year's worth of courage,
I approach him in the Five Spot's hall,
Where he's standing by himself, drinking a coke,
Midnight, between sets.
"Hello, Mr. Monk." He grunts.
"I really liked that last number." He grunts.
But I can't just back off, so I ask,
"What should I think about when I practice *Round Midnight*?"
He half looks at me, pauses, and then says,
In a hoarse low voice,
"The chords, the chords." That's it.
So these last thirty years,
I've been thinking about the chords,
The closed, formal sequence, strict and rich,
The spaces and the solids of a metric.
I should have asked him more:
Annoyed, he might have answered.

THE ICON

A woman, nude to the waist, wearing a skirt
Whose foam-edge is lost in the green, combs her hair
Beneath a tree, an oak, perhaps a laurel.
Her hair is the color of very dark honey
And the smooth skin of her long back is faintly ivory,
The way a Venetian painter would glaze it.

Over a rubble wall that girds her wheatfield
In a field of wild greenery and asphodels
A few goats watch her with their strange cabochon-cut eyes,
And in the laurel tree a couple of warblers
Go about their noisy business; early cicadas too.

She combs her hair out over her nude back
With an old tortoise-shell brush
And looks in a small mirror set on a bough-crook.
Near the tree is a well with a stone cap,
A battered bucket on a rope, and a dry marble basin.
Perhaps she is going to pull water, and wash her hair;
Perhaps she is just combing it, as the morning sun
Flares it in brilliant red points against her ivory back.

If I approach I don't think she'll stop,
I don't think she'll cover her breasts,
Or have words to say to me. Here, perhaps,
Is work for me, a work I don't know how to do -

I have the indolence, the quirky
But not the long concentration.

The right icon held aloft at the right time
Can turn aside the multitudes, can bring harmony
To a room with its small dim icon lamp,
Can be recalled as a spiritual exercise
Or a poetic exercise - a window
Between the two elusive realities.

She puts a couple of pins in her hair, puts away her brush,
Slips on her blouse, and walks across along the wheatfield's edge
Where there are chamomile and poppies. This is
Different now. In the hot sun, perhaps
A bucketful of cold water,
And the sweet, lonesome tug of the well.

OPEN

Open, open

Like chicory flowers in morning

Like the blue in the dome
Of Galla Placidia's
Mediterranean sky.

SAGE LEAF HABITATION

And we were in Athens, kids with the words of that old dream
Biting cleanly through our ignorance.
And we had no money, but it was cheap.
And in front of the Byzantine Museum there were roses,
Red roses in December, unguessed,
And still the light was bright on the famous mountains.
We could see the Acropolis and the temples from the streets
But for four days we were too excited to climb up,
For four days we had to calm down
Seeing it was really there, the ancient walls,
The hallowed marble forms, the wreck of ages.
And our spirit flew over it like gods
To see its perfection, habitable by divinity,
And in the mind it was no ruin
But whole, shining, painted, orienting the world
Of sea and valley and mountain,
Habitable by our goddess of fragrant sage.
Clear forms and a mystery within,
Gold and ivory in the dark, and the pool
        with its floating sage leaf,
And dim light through the thin Parian tiles,
These are insurance for life.

We went in cold drizzle, no one there,
And in the old photograph,

The boy between two Parthenon columns, alone.
And this was before the filthy air rotted the stone,
And the Maidens were marble and strong,
And the air azure, and the sea all sunpoints,
And the mountains green, and the stone white.
And we went the next day, and the next,
Repairing the ruins stone by stone.

But for twenty years of recreation
We did not see the stolen marbles,
And this was the same thing,
Painted marble against its blue background
That made Canova want to start again, too late.
Blue stone, blue sky, blue bay,
Blue for the legends to find their forms.

Age naturally brings its bitterness, the Ionian poets say,
But this icon of reality in the mind
Is not subject to age, they also say, is habitable by gods,
And keeps the eyes open, and thought open,
And the paintings on the marble walls
Waiting to be described
        in a strict and complex metric.
Plato says perfection is a memory,
The poet says an image self-created,
And so the spirit chooses a habitation
On a rock,
        a famous rock with litter of broken stones

sage shrubs flowering among the stones
And the music of a worn mythology.

WEBS

Among the new spring vines,
Among the black boughs newly flowering,
Black Arachne spins her morning web,
Spins and spins again her silver webs,
So that to walk down the stone housepath
Before the sun heats up the stones
You have to take a stick
Not to get wrapped in sticky spider-silk
To which the dew, white and entire, is clinging.

It's hard to find the strands and get them off;
So say: Your fate is not your fate.
Why yours? Why not the mind's that swirls like wind
With every island in the archipelago?
Why not the fig tree's leaning in a field
No one has ploughed for half a century,
Tree unplanted by our hands?

The morning is damp. The webs are in your hair.
"Your fate is not your fate" -
Not that you could avoid it,
Or alter it, or state it,
Or influence the pure and circling thoughts
Of stars' invisible astronomy
By filling in new numbers for sidereal affinities,
Configuring different attributes

To Spring's Hunter and the dainty Sisters.
Two augurs when they meet snort at each other
And tortoise shells are better marked for music.
You're born, you run, you die,
Our sages have kept trying not to say;
And yet we keep on trying
In lines of verse or legacies of cash,
In hillock columns in a sunlight thicket,
To make it something else,
A once upon a time - yes, *once* -
And give it to each other and the world
Of images and networks of desire,
And write twelve books of history
Tragic and packed with incident;
And give sermons that will keep the paid-for pews awake;
And carve in stone the emblems of our ancestors.
And look: trim April's
Buzzing of the bees so loud
That even thoughts go zinging on fast wings
From daisyhead to daisyhead, from blossoms' bough to bough,
A logic not symbolic since
Your fate is not your fate but a mere spume,
A spindrift on a sea of something else
Beyond your competence for celebration.
A cloud passes over, an olive tree flutters,
A hoopoe of Egypt vies with the flowers,
A mountain hawk flashes his red tail
With destiny divine for mice and snakes.

The gods have spun their webs
Which you cannot know.
So let your grief be noble as a stone;
Haven't you been listening to the women?
So let your grief be planted in a field,
The next field up from the high wind-gnarled fig -
Decisions and decisions, and when dull death enwraps you
Before your fate is even half spun out,
So partial and so busy then
And hardly yours the way you are yourself,
And much more than you need,
Oh more fate than your days could ever spin,
More than the Busy Ladies could ever plan for you
Before their black and glittering mythology
Was written down to make your fate a grief.

Yes, the evil keeps on running
And keeps on having to try to run:
Your destiny runs through its interstices
Like purple minnows
Through the thicket of jellyfish tentacles
Drifting amid the sea's sunlight web,
Or like warblers with their silent nestlings
Patient in deep thickets of thorns.

And before you walk back down the stone housepath
All the webs are respun and repaired;
You have to knock them down again

To get back to the porch,

To let your fated day

Begin, and all its labor, love, and grievous error.

NAILS

Things floated heavenly in golden grace
Till Brunelleschi nailed them into place.

THE POGROM AND THE ICON AND THE CORPSE

from the Life of Emmanuel Carson, born Korsunsky.
Odessa, ca. 1905

This was a revolutionary time,
And there were many workers' demonstrations,
Which we the students followed with our own.

This time we students all came out together;
I and my fellows joined the singing crowd,
And as we marched a group of mountain guardsmen,
Yes Cossacks, rushed on us from a side street,
Broke our front line, and started hitting us
With whips. Slightly struck I escaped inside
An unlocked housegate into a safe courtyard.

The pogrom started the next day at dawn.
They came, these hooligans, called the Black Hundred,
Armed with guns; the police assisted them.
They spread throughout the frightened city, shooting
Anyone that they met along their way.
They smashed storefronts and even entered houses.
Hundreds were killed and thousands more were wounded.

In the house right across the street from ours
A priest lived who was sympathetic to
His Jewish neighbors, as we mostly were.

Dressed splendidly in his priestly garb he came
Out to the empty street and held aloft
An icon. "Brother," he told the leader of
The hooligans, "we on this block are Christians."
A blessèd lie. They passed our poor block by.

On many blocks were groups of well-armed workers
And students ready for stiff opposition.
When they encountered them the Cossacks ran.
No coward, I was then too young to fight.

The pogrom lasted three days. Afterwards,
We went off to the cemetery to
Identify the bodies of the slain.
I saw the corpse of one of my school-teachers,
A leader of the self-defense.

These were
A crucial part of my young education,
The pogrom and the icon and the corpse.
When old enough I took sail for New York.
I'm still a socialist, though it went wrong.

NIKE

Girl or perfect goddess
She stoops her strong young body
Casually graceful
To adjust her simple sandal;
Her draperies that fall
In complicated patterns
Evident to the eye
Show through an abstract image
Of wingèd and girl-modest
And fitting nakedness.
From her low parapet
By her Ionic temple
The sea and town and mountains
Are all that they can be
In Attica and beyond.

TOMATOES OF PAROS

Grow these tomatoes rightly
and they will be almost too sweet
but like a kiss
leave your lips burning.

NOTES TO THE POEMS

HARD LIGHT

METONYM

"Two Towers" - off Antiparos' northern tip.

"Strongylon" - deserted islet just west of Antiparos.

"Castro" - town on Siphnos; a kore's torso, now missing, used to lie in the riverbed below it.

AFTER HSIA KUEI

"Hsia Kuei" - 13th century Chinese painter. His masterpiece, "Twelve Views from a Thatched Hut", is in the Nelson Gallery - Atkins Museum.

FOLK SONG

A popular Greek island folk song translated.

FEBRUARY SONNETS

VII "Vorias" - Boreas, the northwind.

"Garbis" - the southwest wind.

NOVEMBER

"cosmos" - a flower.

SEE OFF MOUNTAIN

MIST ON SEE OFF MOUNTAIN

"Tohaku's trees" - the masterpiece of the Japanese painter Tohaku (1539-1610) is the "Pinewood" screen in the Tokyo National Museum; the monochrome trees are in swirling mist.

T'AO CH'IEN ON SEE OFF MOUNTAIN

"T'ao Ch'ien" - Chinese nature poet (365-427), especially of gardens.

"I have my house. . .my inner eye" - loosely adapted from James Robertson Hightower, *The Poetry of T'ao Ch'ien*, p.130.

LOOKING FROM SEE OFF MOUNTAIN TOWARD MT. PISGAH

"Mt. Pisgah" - a mountain near See Off Mountain; also, the mountain whence Moses first saw Canaan.

"Ur" - Mesopotamian city when Abraham was born.

IONIC

THE BEACH OF SAINT IRENE

"ἁντηλιᾱ́" - ant-eliá (pronounced andeelya).

"stood. . .wind" - a fragment of Archilochos of Paros, mid 7th century BCE.

LOOKING FOR TYCHO'S STAR

"Tycho's Star" - visible in Cassiopeia.

"Kepler's supernova" - 1604.

"Queen" - Cassiopeia (Cepheus' wife, Andromeda's mother, Perseus' mother-in law).

"Tyche" - Goddess of Fortune.

FORGOTTEN FORMS: TENOS

"the Greeks held out" - Tenos, under the Venetians from 1207, was the last of the Cyclades to fall to the Turks, in 1714.

"her church" - church of the Virgin of Good Tidings, it houses her icon famed for miraculous cures.

DELOS

"Whence boats. . .birthing" - in the Periclean Age, it was forbidden to give birth or to die on sacred Delos; the likely were taken to Rheneia.

THERA: FUTURE FIRE

"Naked. . .pumice stone" - from Seferis' "Santorini".

"Nea Kaimeni" - Volcanic lava flows in 1707-11 raised a new islet in Thera's bay; its name means "new burnt one."

NYMPH OF SERIPHOS

"Aseid, Napaea", etc. - nymph types.

"God's gold/on waiting thighs" - Danae, Perseus' mother.

THE GODS WITHDRAW

"Aphrodite's inimitable gesture" - from H.D.'s *Helen in Egypt*.

"love. . .oak" - a fragment of Sappho of Lesbos.

"praise. . .verity's" - from Pound's Cavalcanti.

ODE IN DAWN SUNLIGHT

Epigraph - "O godly aether and many-winged birds,/springs of rivers, seawaves'/numberless laughter, all-mother earth,/and all-seeing circle of the sun, I call upon you": Prometheus' first speech.

"Iktinos" - architect of Apollo's temple at Bassai and of the Parthenon; invented the Corinthian capital.

"turn and counterturn and stand" - strophe, antistrophe, epode.

CAPE SOUNION

"Kouros" - a kouros from Sounion is in the Athens museum.

COVE

The two quotations are from Plato's *Timaeus* and *Phaedrus*.

FROGS AND SWALLOWS

UNLACONIC GREEN

"Taygetus" - high mountain by Sparta.

"shake your fearsome crests at them" - translated from Tyrtaios (7th century BCE).

ATARGATIS OF ASCALON

Ascalon, the Philistine city-state, according to Herodotus, had the most ancient temple of Aphrodite Urania, or Atargatis.

MONK AND POET

Both quotations are from Hesiod's *Works and Days*.

TO DELPHIC APOLLO

"Apostate king" - The emperor Julian (332-363).

THE CHERRY TREES AT HAGIOS IOANNES KAPAROS

St. John of Kaparos is owned and lovingly tended by Mr. John Kaparos, on Paros.

DESPOTIKON

Despotikon is a small deserted island west of Paros.

VILLA ROSPIGLIOSI

The Villa Rospigliosi is in the hills outside of Pistoia.

THREE TRAGIC POEMS

"ὤμοι . . . / a mortal blow" - from the *Agamemnon*, as is the next bit of Greek.

"πολλὰ τὰ δεινὰ / Many things" - from the *Antigone*.

"Bird you sing. . ./. . .the sea" - translated from the big chorus of *Iphigeneia in Taurus*.

"τί τὸ σοφὸν / What is wisdom" - from the *Bacchae*.

THE TEMPLE AND THE DOLPHIN

PRELUDE

"Spyridon, Nicholas. . .Sozon" - saints who protect mariners.

OXYRHYNCHUS

In 1897 the dumps of Oxyrhynchus in the Sahara, a town till then unknown, yielded a large number of discarded Greek papyri.

DANAE'S DREAM

Acrisius received the oracle that his daughter Danae was destined to bear a son that would kill him, so he locked her up in a brazen dungeon. Zeus saw her, lusted, and came unto her in a golden rain, which impregnated her. When her child, Perseus, was born, Acrisius sent them to sea sealed in a little ark. They arrived safely in Seriphos. Perseus, after beheading Medusa and unchaining Andromeda, accidentally killed his grandfather with a discus. The opening lines somewhat describe Titian's painting in the Prado. Sometimes the Renaissance pretended this scene prefigured the Annunciation.

ARION AND THE DOLPHIN

Archilochos supposedly invented the iamb. "O how I long to touch Neoboule's hand" is perhaps the first known personal love lyric. The story of Arion and the dolphin, retold here, is from Herodotus.

ICON

PHOENIX

The measurement is correct.

THE CITY

"the elder Bellini brother,/Will paint his delicate portrait" - now in London's National Gallery.

"Holy Wisdom" - the church of Saint Sophia.

"Constantine Paleologus" - the last Byzantine emperor heroically died defending the city; his body was not found.

"THE CHORDS, THE CHORDS"

The great Thelonius Monk often played New York's Five Spot in the early 60s.

OPEN

"Galla Placidia" - Emperor Honorius' sister erected a small building in Ravenna, *ca.* 450, whose magnificent mosaics are predominantly blue.

NIKE

The exquisite relief is in the Acropolis museum. Also see the photograph "Nike" by Elizabeth Carson.